Internationalist perspectives seem to
world needs them most. This can be ch
leaders to choose bold responses base
nie's short but powerful book makes a co.............
Investment based on statutory contributions (rather than patronising "aid" from rich to poor countries) as a necessary element to deal with the challenges we face.

Jayati Ghosh
Professor of Economics,
Jawaharlal Nehru University, New Delhi

Most people think of foreign aid in terms of humanitarian assistance. Jonathan Glennie has bolder ambitions. He suggests using aid for global public investments that make everyone better off. With COVID-19 underlining the inequalities and unsustainability of the current structure of development finance, big new ideas are needed. That is what this book provides.

Homi Kharas
Senior Fellow, Brookings Institution

At a time when reforming international co-operation has become a matter of urgency and all perspectives should be heard, Jonathan Glennie's thought-provoking book sets the stage for a paradigm shift, with its proposal for global public investment.

Mario Pezzini
Director, OECD Development Centre

Jonathan Glennie brilliantly recommends the transformation of foreign aid into Global Public Investment and, in alignment with the Sustainable Development Goals, he advocates for a universal and sustainable approach, to renew our understanding of the international system. A reading must!

Patti Londoño
Former Colombian foreign minister

It is hard not to feel overwhelmed by the relentless onslaught of current global events. The planet that sustains us is barely coping with extreme weather events, bush fires, and the decimation of wildlife. Conflicts and other human-made disasters are driving mass movements of populations to seek safety, refuge and better livelihoods and gains in poverty reduction are in serious threat of being reversed. The Covid-19 pandemic could not have hit at a worse time. Nonetheless, the amalgamation of these events could be the catalyst for the change we need to address these challenges – and in *The Future of Aid: Global Public Investment*, Jonathan Glennie, persuasively, provides important insights and critical analyses to deliberate on how we might do this... Based on scholarly reviews and dialogue, *The Future of Aid: Global Public Investment* is a demonstration of a rare skill in an academic author; the ability to combine fairly dense ideas with engaging prose to make the text accessible to a broad audience. It is timely and required reading for those tasked to engage in international public finance.

Pascale Allotey
Director, United Nations University
International Institute for Global Health

This publication is timely and necessary. It not only provides very practical ideas on how countries could come together to fight immediate global challenges such as the Covid-19 pandemic, but also offers a framework on how to sustainably finance the SDGs. It is a first of its kind and should shape global policy and development co-operation in years to come. It is a must read for any policy maker and practitioner!

Vitalice Meja
Executive Director, Reality of Aid Africa

Jonathan Glennie revives the conversation on development cooperation at the right time. The world can no longer be seen as a patchwork of countries, but as a global community working towards common goals. From the objectives to the practices of development cooperation, this book presents the key areas of debate and the types of creative thinking needed in the future. The book is an invitation to the development community to re-imagine itself by questioning some strongly held beliefs about international cooperation. The world has changed from how it was seen at the beginning of this century. This is a must-read for anyone interested in a new international response to global problems.

Andrea Ordóñez
Director, Southern Voice

By boldly thinking outside the box and challenging the conventional wisdom regarding aid, this timely book offers an entirely new approach to how we should confront the global challenges of the 21st century. Calling for a sweeping change in the objectives, concepts and practice of development finance, it will garner support from scholars and practitioners alike.

André de Mello e Souza
Senior Researcher, Institute for Applied
Economic Research, Rio de Janeiro

Global social justice is the ultimate global public good. We need Global Public Investment to make global social justice happen. This brilliant book explains how. You should read it.

Gorik Ooms
Honorary Professor of Global Health Law &
Governance, London School of Hygiene &
Tropical Medicine

Abandoning the hierarchical and demeaning concept of "aid" for the dignified and responsible concept of Global Public Investment, Glennie shifts focus from national priorities to the global good. GPI is an exciting new concept in which public funds are a proactive and long-term investment in the common endeavour of development.

Nora Lester Murad
Founder, Dalia Association, Ramallah

Covid-19 threatens to plunge millions of people back into poverty. We need unprecedented ambition to respond to this extraordinary crisis, and to other challenges such as climate change. This book sets out one part of the answer.

Andy Sumner
Professor of International Development,
King's College, London

Today's world is very different from that in which international aid was created. New international powers have emerged, the range of official and private providers has enlarged, and new and more complex issues threaten our future progress and wellbeing. In accordance, we are obliged to go beyond aid and transit to a more ambitious and inclusive system of public collective action at the international level. Jonathan Glennie draws up some of the required components of this alternative approach. In an illuminating book, he offers to us a fresh view on this topic, with defiant proposals and illuminating insights.

José Antonio Alonso
Professor of Applied Economics,
Complutense University, Madrid

For those interested in international development, this book could hardly be more timely. The traditional model of rich north, poor south, and the aid paradigm which was part of it, suffered a major body-blow with the global financial crash of 2008/9. Coronavirus is a more recent and powerful incentive to think about the world and the relationship between its constituent parts in a different way. This thoughtful and provocative volume does not pretend to have all the answers. It is a beginning, an invaluable contribution to the thinking required to set us on the path to finding the concessional resources needed to address the global challenges - enshrined within the Sustainable Development Goals - which we must address urgently, and together.

Myles Wickstead
Visiting Professor, King's College,
London, and former UK Ambassador to Ethiopia

The Future of Aid: Global Public Investment usefully exposes gaps between old paradigms and new realities in international development cooperation. While arguing to retire the concept of "foreign aid," Glennie maintains that international public finance is a unique resource for greater equity and sustainability, amidst increasingly diverse financing sources and complex risks like climate change and Covid-19. His proposals for adapting development finance to meet the ambition of the SDGs are certain to stimulate thinking and debate.

Navid Hanif
Director, Financing for Sustainable
Development Office, UNDESA

A new vision for global public finance has been long overdue. Jonathan Glennie's concept of Global Public Investment (GPI) comes at the right time, when we urgently need new ideas to shape the future of public finance. Poverty, inequality, fragility and access to food, water and other essential resources remain critical headwinds the world must tackle to become sustainable and stable. None of them can be tackled without adequate financing. They require new international financing mechanisms which build on the past but respond to the future. GPI is an idea whose time has come.

Harpinder Collacott
Executive Director, Development Initiatives

The change of approach this book is calling for fits perfectly in the spirit that guided the development of Agenda 2030, with solidarity as the backdrop. Global Public Investment is a platform meriting proper consideration... and a potential rallying point as we plan ahead how to reconstruct the socio-economic fabric after the pandemic.

Francisco Songane
Former Minister of Health of Mozambique

Aid is obsolete. But, in an era of pandemic, climate change and rising inequality effective international cooperation is an existential issue for humanity. In *The Future of Aid: Global Public Investment* Jonathan Glennie lays out both a new paradigm and a practical agenda for international public financing to achieve social justice and sustainability. The arguments are radical but feasible - a 'must read' for anyone interested in global development.

David Hulme
Executive Director, Global Development Institute,
University of Manchester

Jonathan Glennie has long been one of the most original and insightful voices within the aid world. In this revolutionary book he brilliantly insists that we raise the level of our ambition in the way we fund public goods and services globally. The era of aid is over. In these pages Glennie sketches out the beginnings of a new paradigm for a fairer, greener and more stable world.

Simon Reid-Henry
Director, Institute for the Humanities and
Social Sciences, Queen Mary, University of London

The world needs to build back better following the unprecedented Covid-19 crisis. This will require an extraordinary amount of resources in all countries. Jonathan Glennie's innovative concept of Global Public Investment offers the best opportunity to date to succeed in this vital effort.

Christoph Benn
Director, Global Health Diplomacy,
Joep Lange Institute

This book articulates what many intuitively feel but few say out loud: that aid needs reformed, increased and maintained for the long term. Not charity, but smart investment in a more just and sustainable world. Glennie eloquently lays out a new vision for the necessary international public finance required. If you are serious about fighting inequality and climate change this is a must read.

David McNair
Executive Director, Global Policy,
The ONE Campaign

The COVID-19 pandemic should have shown how international cooperation for the provision of global public goods and fighting inequalities is more needed than ever. But it didn't; instead, we witness a growing noise about deglobalization. That's why Glennie's *The Future of Aid: Global Public Investment* hits home. It reframes the development agenda, tackling its goals, means and narratives. Glennie's book brings the fight against inequality to the fore, as the ultimate goal of international cooperation for development. Moreover, it makes the compelling case that Global Public Investment (GPI) is the way forward for providing global public goods and, therefore, to contribute to a fairer distribution of wealth. *The Future of Aid* goes beyond an abstract universalism and a dyadic notion of responsibility. A mitigated universalism underpins its narrative, combining two principles adopted by Southern countries: differentiation and mutuality. Glennie's vision stresses the idea that progressive differentiation (every state should contribute according to its capacities), is based on self-interest (the contribution will, ultimately, benefit the contributor). In a time of growing suspicion of multilateralism, Glennie's work on GPI is a most needed roadmap to tackle intractable challenges and to revive the 2030 Agenda.

Paulo Esteves
Director, BRICS Policy Center

The international community, bracing with the changes in the development cooperation landscape, has been in a reflective mood in recent times. The Covid-19 pandemic has provided a compelling boost to this process of rethinking. It is now widely recognised that novel ideas and gutsy initiatives are the need of the day to evolve a more effective global arrangement of collaboration for sustainable development. At this very opportune moment, Jonathan Glennie has come forward with the ambitious proposal of transforming the traditional aid regime to "global public investment". His analytical narrative touches upon issues related to motivation and incentives as well as sourcing and governance. Discerning readers will find the book engaging and intriguing.

Debapriya Bhattacharya
Distinguished Fellow, Centre for
Policy Dialogue, and former Bangladesh
Ambassador to WTO and UN

With passion and academic proficiency, Glennie calls to replace the "aid" paradigm of international cooperation i.e. transfers from affluent nations to underprivileged ones, with an internationalist democratic approach cemented on the belief in the capacities of peoples to collectively work on an equal footing for the common good of all: Global Public Investment. Repairing a ship in the midst of a tempest requires not charity between those in upper and lower decks, but the full investment of everyone's actions and expertise. As the pandemic has shown, for each nation, its economic wellbeing and health of its population crucially depend on the fate of other nations. Practitioners, policy makers, academics and students of international development and global affairs will benefit enormously from this book; the world too, if politicians in power heed Glennie's advice.

Juan Carlos Moreno-Brid
Professor of Economics, UNAM, and
co-founder of the World Economic Association

I am so excited about this book! It's the first really inspired take on the changes we need to make in the aid and global development system I've seen this year. As countries struggle to address health, social and economic fall-outs of the COVID-19 pandemic, one thing remains clear: the ideals of equality, dignity and justice are as relevant now as they were during civil rights and anti-colonial movements of the previous century. We urgently need governments across the world to reinforce international obligations to advance human rights and civic freedoms, and ensure that civil society is an equal partner in the achievement of an equal and sustainable world. As this book rightly argues, rethinking aid as a global public investment is critical if we are to secure our undeniably inter-dependent future.

Lysa John
Secretary-General, Civicus
(global alliance of civil society)

Glennie offers a timely and critical examination of the "aid paradigm" that has governed global cooperation for most of the 20th century. This book is his manifesto for remaking foreign aid to address new political realities and development challenges. A book for aid theorists and policy practitioners alike, he offers a powerful rationale for concessional public financial transfers: international solidarity that serves all of our collective interests as co-inhabitants of planet Earth. At the same time, his idealism is tempered by a keen realism of the geopolitics of foreign aid, including the ways it must build diplomatic bridges and tear down 'us and them' mentalities. A book for our times that is bound to both provoke and stimulate in equal measure.

Nilima Gulrajani
Senior Research Fellow, Overseas
Development Institute

"First and most important thing to say is that I love this! The basic argument is both timely and visionary – and if taken up genuinely world changing on a massive scale – and I think it has a real chance of being taken up. I think it's an incredibly important book, with the potential to really make a difference. It's also very well written – conceptually packaged clearly and persuasively – and written in a credible and intelligent, but also accessible and readable, style".

Martin Drewry
Director, Health Poverty Action

The Future of Aid

International cooperation has never been more needed, but the current system of "aid" is outdated and ineffective. *The Future of Aid* calls for a wholesale restructuring of the aid project, a totally new approach fit for the challenges of the 21st century: Global Public Investment.

Across the world, billions of people are struggling to get by in unequal and unsustainable societies, and international public finance, which should be part of the answer, is woefully deficient. Engagingly written by a well-known expert in the field, *The Future of Aid* calls for a series of paradigm shifts.

- From a narrow focus on poverty to a broader attack on inequality and unsustainability.
- From seeing international public money as a temporary last resort, to valuing it as a permanent force for good.
- From North-South transfers to a collective effort, with all paying in and all benefitting.
- From outdated post-colonial institutions to representative decision-making.
- From the othering and patronising language of "foreign aid", to the empowering concept of Global Public Investment.

Ten years ago, in *The Trouble with Aid*, Jonathan Glennie highlighted the dangers of aid dependency and the importance of looking beyond aid. Now he calls for a revolution in the way that we think about the role of public money to back up our ambitious global objectives. In the wake of the Covid-19 crisis, it is time for a new era of internationalism.

Jonathan Glennie is a writer and campaigner on human rights, sustainable development and poverty. His work looks in particular at the changing nature of international cooperation as dominant paradigms and global relationships evolve. He has held senior positions in several international organisations, including Save the Children, Christian Aid, and Ipsos. He has published two previous books on aid (*The Trouble With Aid: Why Less Could Mean More for Africa* and *Aid, Growth and Poverty,* with Andy Sumner) and helped set up *The Guardian's* Global Development website. As a consultant, he has worked with governments, international agencies and civil society organisations as they renew their strategies for a new era. He lives in Colombia.

The Future of Aid
Global Public Investment

Jonathan Glennie

Routledge
Taylor & Francis Group

LONDON AND NEW YORK

First published 2021
by Routledge
2 Park Square, Milton Park, Abingdon, Oxon OX14 4RN

and by Routledge
52 Vanderbilt Avenue, New York, NY 10017

*Routledge is an imprint of the Taylor & Francis Group, an
Informa business*

British Library Cataloguing-in-Publication Data
A catalogue record for this book is available from the
British Library

Library of Congress Cataloguing-in-Publication Data
Names: Glennie, Jonathan, author.
Title: The future of aid : global public investment / Jonathan Glennie.
Description: New York : Routledge, 2020. | Includes bibliographical
references and index. |
Identifiers: LCCN 2020028427 (print) | LCCN 2020028428 (ebook) | ISBN
9780367359324 (hardback) | ISBN 9780367404970 (paperback) | ISBN
9780429356384 (ebook)
Subjects: LCSH: Public investments--Social aspects. | International
cooperation--Social aspects. | Social change. | Globalization--Social
aspects.
Classification: LCC HC79.P83 G54 2020 (print) | LCC HC79.P83 (ebook) |
DDC 332.67/252--dc23
LC record available at https://lccn.loc.gov/2020028427
LC ebook record available at https://lccn.loc.gov/2020028428

ISBN: 978-0-367-35932-4 (hbk)
ISBN: 978-0-367-40497-0 (pbk)
ISBN: 978-0-429-35638-4 (ebk)

Typeset in Times New Roman
by KnowledgeWorks Global Ltd.

Printed and bound by CPI Group (UK) Ltd, Croydon, CR0 4YY

Contents

Tables

Foreword

The Covid-19 pandemic threatens to set back development progress for a generation as its health, social and economic impacts play out. But in this critical moment, it is also clearer than ever that serious structural changes are needed to safeguard communities around the world, and the planet itself. As inequality widens and threats to global health and sustainability multiply, so also the progress made on reducing extreme poverty has been halted – the numbers living in extreme poverty are rising for the first time this century. With growing nationalism in many countries, we need now to strengthen our discourse of solidarity and shared responsibility. The changing nature of geopolitics is conducive to doing that as the voices of the Global South continue to strengthen in the international arena.

This is the context in which this book proposes a new vision for development cooperation. The Sustainable Development Goals (SDGs) offer a bold global framework through which to address common challenges and build a coherent response, but we still haven't worked out how to safeguard and enhance the provision of public goods and services across the world. Clearly, the current financial system is not working. Building on the best of "aid", Jonathan Glennie suggests a series of paradigm shifts to modernise our approach. Those shifts include raising ambitions from the level of the Millennium Development Goals (MDGs) to that of the more comprehensive SDGs, emphasising the unique value of concessional international public finance as a complement to other sources of development finance, recognising the shifting geography of development cooperation to which all the world's countries now contribute one way or another and suggesting governance arrangements to reflect that. We should also insist on a new narrative to replace the old-fashioned and misleading language of "donors" and "aid".

Many of these changes are already underway, thanks to the hard work and vision of many working in governments, civil society and international organisations around the world. This book pushes us to go further in redesigning this crucial sector for a new era, one now in flux as never before as the Covid-19 crisis continues. Never has internationalism been more needed than today. Never have the opportunities been so great, nor the price of failure so devastating. I hope the ideas in this book will provoke new ways of thinking and contributing which will help us navigate through our present challenges and build a fairer and more sustainable world.

Rt Hon. Helen Clark
Former Administrator of UNDP
Former Prime Minister of New Zealand

Helen Clark was Prime Minister of New Zealand for three successive terms from 1999-2008. She was the first woman to become Prime Minister following a General Election in New Zealand and the second woman to serve as Prime Minister. From 2009 until 2017 she served as Administrator of the United Nations Development Programme, the first woman to lead the organisation. Helen serves on a number of advisory boards and commissions, including in the capacity of Chair of the Boards of the Extractive Industries Transparency Initiative and the Partnership for Maternal, Newborn and Child Health, and of the Advisory Board of UNESCO's Global Education Monitoring Report. She is also the Patron of The Helen Clark Foundation which has been established as a think tank to support evidence-informed debate on issues about which Helen has been passionate all her life.

Acknowledgments

This book is the culmination of 7 years' work and collaboration with many brilliant people. Most notably I must thank Gail Hurley who would have been a co-author had it not been for other commitments. Much of the thinking in this book is hers, and there are chunks of text scattered throughout which she originally drafted. Other important collaborators along the way have been José Antonio Alonso, Francisco Sagasti, Alioune Sall, Simon Reid-Henry and Rathin Roy. Special thanks to Peter van Rooijen and Anton Ofield-Kerr who injected much needed energy into this work just at the right moment. Thanks to all those present at numerous consultations, retreats and presentations all over the world, physically and remotely, who provided great ideas and critiques as we honed this ambitious and original idea, particularly the Global Fund Advocacy Network. Thanks to all at the Joep Lange Institute and International Civil Society Support. Comments have been gratefully received from, among others, Richard Manning, Nilima Gulrajani, Julia Greenberg, Harpinder Collacott, Thomas Pogge, Guido Schmidt-Traub, Joanne Carter, Mike Podmore, Jamila Headley, Gorik Ooms, Lilianne Ploumen, Myles Wickstead, Christoph Benn, David Barr, David McNair, Midnight Poonkasetwattana, Ellen Croes, Khalil Elouardighi, Jamie Drummond, Rita da Costa, Rachel Ong, Pablo Yanguas, Homi Kharas, Ben Phillips, Juan Carlos Lozano, Martin Drewry, Natalie Sharples, Hannah Ryder, Andy Sumner. Any errors are, of course, my own.

Like any author I am aware of all the deficiencies in this book, and I don't doubt that readers will come out the other end with significantly more questions than answers. I wanted to write a short readable book, and that has meant relegating some major topics to no more than a few lines and leaving some important issues unresolved. This is the beginning of an idea still in its infancy, a provocation to build something new, rather than a finalised, detailed policy paper. And that is as it should be. I hope that many more people will add their views and knowledge to make this idea bigger and better. I look forward to being part of a movement for change that builds a more modern and effective system to pay for the things we all care about, wherever in the world we live.

This book is dedicated to my wife, Victoria, my companion and inspiration, who daily reminds me to believe that a better world is possible, and to my children, Daniel, Solomon and Sofia, who I hope will help build it.

All proceeds from this book will be donated to the Inter-Church Justice and Peace Commission (CIJP) which works tirelessly for human rights in Colombia.

Glossary of key terms

Development cooperation Development cooperation is that part of international cooperation which is specifically for development purposes.

Financing for Development/Development Finance (FFD) Includes all monies that can help finance development (official and private, concessional or under market conditions, international and domestic). This can include remittances and foreign direct investment (FDI) and domestic resources such as taxes and local private sector investment.

Foreign Aid A broad and imprecise concept, often (wrongly) used synonymously with ODA. It refers to the transfer of resources from one country to another, usually under concessional terms.

Global Public Investment (GPI) A new term proposed in this book to describe concessional IPF with a defined purpose: to support internationally agreed developmental objectives (e.g. the SDGs).

International public finance (IPF) A term used to cover all types of publicly sourced money transferred internationally. Not necessarily concessional and not necessarily intended to promote development.

Official development assistance (ODA) A technical term referring to contributions made by OECD member countries. There is a strict definition regarding the concessionality of these flows and their purpose.

South-South Cooperation (SSC) Support offered by countries of the Global South to other countries in the Global South. This support is often, but by no means always, financial.

1   The beginning of the end?

A pandemic that threatens everyone and has shut down everything. A once in a century economic collapse that is casting millions of people into unemployment. Rising social tension. The Covid-19 crisis requires a huge and urgent response to save lives and to help billions of people out of economic hardship. But while it throws a sharp relief on global inequality and the urgent changes we need to see, in terms of what the world needs in the long term it changes nothing. We have long known that we need far more money, better distributed, to support global prosperity, including global public goods. And everyone knows that our current decision-making ("governance") systems are not fit for purpose at the global level. We are driving a broken-down car. Without any fuel.

The world needs a coherent, ambitious and effective global response to the multiple challenges it faces, including but not limited to the Covid-19 outbreak. We have never needed one more. But what we have is incoherence, lack of vision and, inevitably therefore, weak and ineffective attempts at cooperation for our common good. And that isn't just because global leaders are failing. The way we have been taught to think about global cooperation is outdated, and global institutions are struggling. The pervasive "aid" paradigm is preventing the world's nations from taking the steps we desperately need to reform and rebuild our world for the 21st century. Rather than planning for the expansion of cooperation that is so clearly required, the "aid" system is, bizarrely, set for gradual shutdown over the next few years. This shutdown is built into the theory of aid, a bit like the obsolescence famously built into old-fashioned light-bulbs. Maybe not immediately, because there are still a few more things that aid can help with, still a few pockets of poverty. And we will always need to throw some money at emergencies from time to time. But we are being prepared for the end of foreign aid as a core part of global development. Any number of quotes could demonstrate this.

Take Donald Kaberuka, a former President of the African Development Bank, who said, "Aid is not successful unless it has a sell-by date. If aid does not stop, it will have failed".[1]

Barack Obama put it succinctly (as one would expect): "Foreign Assistance is not an end in itself. The purpose of aid must be to create the conditions where it is no longer needed".[2]

According to Paul Collier, an influential British academic, "There is basically no role for international development cooperation in middle-income countries".[3] Given that almost all countries are now either middle- or high-income, and that most of the 30 or so remaining low-income countries are expected to "graduate" to a higher status in the coming years, that's quite a limited vision for the future of development cooperation. It seems that sending money abroad to help other parts of the world, an activity which has lasted over seven decades, is on its way out.

This has been the common view in the aid business for years. It's the logical consequence of traditional assumptions about aid and the implication of the economic theories that have been rolled out to support it. It's also the expectation of the taxpaying public whose money is being spent.

Whether you are a citizen of a "donor" country, still feeling the effects of austerity from the 2008 crash and preparing for the inevitable economic downturn prompted by Covid-19 lockdowns, or a citizen of a "recipient" country whose economy feels like it is taking off for the first time in living memory and keen to reduce dependence on the Global North; whether you believe the aid era has been quite successful in promoting development but has now "done its job", or that aid has been an unqualified failure that's done more harm than good (or if you have a more nuanced view, understanding aid's pros and cons); whether you think the hole left behind by aid can be best filled by more domestic taxes, or by increased private sector investment, or by remittances from migrants, or by philanthropy, or some mix of all them; whatever side of the political spectrum you sit on, from populist right to internationalist left – you are unlikely to disagree with the notion that aid is a temporary fix for a temporary problem, a fillip to kick-start growth in sluggish contexts, a humane response to extreme and unusual challenges, to be reduced and eventually ended as people and countries become wealthier. That's what you have been told your whole life.

And that is exactly what appears to be happening. To take one of many examples, the UK ended its aid programme to India back in

2012, saying that aid to India could not "continue forever" and that a new relationship based on trade, not aid, would now be put in place[4]– no matter that India is one of the world's poorest countries where, today, almost a decade later, fewer than one in ten infants are fed a minimum acceptable diet.[5] Other "strong candidates" for aid reductions, according to one former UK aid minister, include poor African countries such as Ghana, Uganda and Zambia,[6] despite having maternal mortality rates at around 300 per 100,000 births – in the UK the rate is just seven per 100,000.[7] Whole continents have now been pushed off the aid map: aid to most of Latin America has long since been ended by many of the main donor countries, due to its lack of "extremely poor" people. The message to the public in wealthy countries is clear: "Don't worry, poverty is ending, just one last push and we will be able to finish with this aid experiment. Then your taxes will be spent in your own country again".

Those of us who have worked in international development for a long time tend to have been trained with this as a basic assumption. In fact, one of our favourite mantras has always been that the job of aid is to "do itself out of a job" (as Kaberuka and Obama imply in the quotes above). But, as you have probably guessed by now, a growing number of us don't think that any more. As we have watched the world evolve in the 21st century we have become convinced that the era of largescale public investment in international progress and development is not coming to an end. Quite the contrary: it is only just beginning. In fact, it has taken on a new importance as humanity grapples with rising inequality and unsustainability, to add to the central challenge of poverty. The Covid-19 crisis has demonstrated this more starkly than ever making now the moment to push for an historic change in the way we view international financial cooperation.

It is quite obvious that we need more public money at the international level to spend on crucial joint global objectives. But we can't just have more of the same. There are fundamental problems with the way "foreign aid" is currently understood and managed that make it seem like a 20th century anomaly stuck in a very different 21st century reality. Most people in the aid industry recognise this and many are actively trying to change things. But attempts to update the sector have so far been piecemeal and confused. Everyone is talking about the need for reform, but no-one has much of an idea what that reform should look like. This book provides a framework for a new approach. It is not perfect, and there is much to do to hone the idea, but I hope it inspires a new generation of internationalists to understand the importance of public spending for international development in a new way.

The first thing we need to do is to drop the word "aid" and the baggage that surrounds it. Rather than think of the money countries spend beyond their borders as "aid" for some faraway others, we should see it as an investment in our common global good, the price of a better world. That's why I propose a new term – **Global Public Investment**, or **GPI** for short. I hope to challenge long-standing beliefs and new-fangled myths at the heart of today's "aid" narrative, and draw on research and practice already underway to suggest ways to build a new system that works for the global common good and puts the poorest first.

According to conventional "aid" theories, poorer countries have a gap in their finances that needs filling by richer countries. That's partly right and very important, but it is not the full story. Concessional international public finance (IPF) also has certain characteristics that make it a unique type of finance even when it is not filling financial gaps. It is motivated by international solidarity, not national priorities, or profit. It is often available when other monies are not. It is usually accompanied by great expertise. These qualities are as important as the quantity, which is why we need to be spending *more* concessional IPF on reducing poverty and inequality, not less, and *more* also on promoting planetary sustainability.

Spending more public money, more effectively, is not the only thing needed to support development internationally. Far from it. The causes of poverty, inequality and unsustainability are structural, and it is impossible for international public money alone to make a real difference in the absence of policies to transform the economy and society, nationally and globally. So it is important not to *overclaim* for what **Global Public Investment** will be able achieve. It is just a piece of the puzzle, but it is an important piece. Useful attempts to push people to think "beyond aid" to more structural issues are in danger of morphing into excuses to drop the financial part of international cooperation altogether. That would be a grave mistake. We need to keep on fighting for structural changes to make our world fairer – but we also need to ensure redistributive and forward-looking public investments for the medium and long term, because structural change is a long process. While tech billionaires work up plans to send people off to live on Mars, **Global Public Investment** should become a mainstay of our collective efforts to make our planet a fairer, safer, greener and healthier home.

"Aid" – an obsolete approach

This book is going to say that increasing amounts of well-spent **Global Public Investment** will be needed to help achieve our global objectives and, frankly, save the planet. This central contention is based on copious evidence that IPF, when spent well, really can help improve millions of lives. But aid (and other similar kinds of spending) has not been without its critics, and rightly so. While it has often been a vital part of development success, it has also sometimes held back progress.

The world's grand experiment with foreign aid began in the aftermath of a devastating world war. The vision behind it is perhaps best articulated by US president Harry Truman in his Point Four address in 1949 which called for "a bold new program for making the benefits of our scientific advances and industrial progress available for the improvement and growth of underdeveloped areas". Aid has been through many changes over the years: from the "big push" rhetoric of the 1960s, the setting of the 0.7% of Gross National Income (GNI) target for the wealthy Organisation for Economic Cooperation and Development (OECD) countries in 1970, structural adjustment in the 1980s and 1990s and then the era of the Millennium Development Goals (MDGs) for the first 15 years of this century which saw a renewed focus on social sector spending. At different times and in different places, foreign aid has focused on everything from infrastructure, agriculture, manufacturing, conflict prevention, human rights, women's equality, health and education, institution building, environmental protection, emergency response and pretty much everything else. The current fad is using aid to leverage private capital in support of economic development.

But while aid has had many faces, the basic narrative has remained unchanged. Aid is a transfer of money from richer "developed" countries to poorer "developing" ones. Aid is a charitable endeavour, with self-described "donors" calling the shots on how and where it is spent. Aid is temporary support to help foreign countries out of exceptional difficulties related to poverty and poor governance while other financial options, like taxes and private investment, are unavailable. Aid will eventually end when the economies of recipient countries are big enough, leaving aid departments (from JICA in Japan to USAID in the US) to close their doors for the last time. There might be a small residual left over for emergencies, but the many billions of dollars currently at play will be a thing of the past.

This approach is out of date, given how different today's global reality is to the one in which Truman gave his famous speech, and it is beyond time to question the fundamentals that underpin today's aid project. The challenges facing the world have evolved and expanded. Eradicating extreme poverty remains the central focus of international cooperation, but it can no longer be the only priority. As living standards improve in many parts of the world, so do expectations, and ambitions for human welfare are rightly being recalibrated. Meanwhile, the environmental challenge, from saving forests to cleaning up the oceans and, ultimately, the need for humanity to address climate change is more urgent than ever. Add to that a list of international policy issues that seems to be getting longer all the time– think peace and security, controlling communicable diseases (most recently Covid-19), science and research, international tax matters, organised crime to name a few – and you have a long shopping list of top priority items requiring a significantly sized wallet. Rapid technological advance creates opportunities but it also raises risks and uncertainty. One contextual factor remains persistently, perniciously, the same: the structural inequalities that favour wealth and privilege remain fully intact, with many indicators of inequality worsening in recent decades.

The good news is that the opportunities for successful international response to these challenges has also transformed, and new ways of working abound. In this era of hyper-globalisation, countries are more closely connected than ever before, expanding opportunities for states and societies to collaborate on issues of shared concern. As historically poorer countries do better economically, all countries are increasingly contributing to solving the world's problems. The fact that some leading countries are currently going through a kind of blinkered isolation does not change these fundamentals.

Just over a decade ago I wrote a book called *"The Trouble with Aid: Why less could mean more for Africa"* which argued that high levels of aid dependency over long periods of time were proving downright harmful. The arrival of large amounts of cash in relatively poor countries can distort economies and undermine the development of accountable and effective democratic institutions, and many of the policy conditions that have been attached to aid in the past have often done more harm than good. And it's no surprise, not least because the motives behind foreign aid are complex. Aid is often genuinely charitable, but it has also been used to bully recipient countries to adopt particular policies against their will and can be a weapon in the armoury of powerful countries to impose their will globally – this was particularly the case during the Cold War in which East and West fought for geopolitical dominance. So, building on the analyses of African experts, I suggested that African countries should do all they could to reduce dependency i.e. the amount of aid they received relative to the size of their economies.[8]

Many of us have spent our careers calling for the international development sector to move on from its obsession with aid to more profound structural issues – such as mobilising domestic resources through better taxation, directing private money to sustainable development and engaging on climate change policy, trade rules, land rights, the arms trade, to name a few – and we have been quite successful. The so-called "beyond aid" agenda, which emphasises that countries demonstrate their commitment to development and poverty reduction by addressing a whole range of policies, not just aid, has become embedded in the last decade or so, and the last thing we now want to do is lose sight of these more fundamental development policy choices by over-focusing on financial transfers.[9]

But we face a different problem now to the one we faced 15 years ago. Back then, there was an *over*-emphasis on aid and a consequent *under*-emphasis on more fundamental ways in which the international community can support development. But today, while a "beyond aid" focus remains crucial, the importance of continued financial transfers is being subtly edged off the scene. As the mainstream development discourse ever more boldly extols the virtues of non-aid policies, the baby is being thrown out with the bath water. The unique contribution made by IPF to progressive causes and public goods is being glossed over, with unrealistic expectations being placed on other forms of finance (private, philanthropic, domestic) that have very different qualities and drivers. To be blunt, some governments are using the "beyond aid" rhetoric to retreat from their international obligations to redistribute some of their accumulated wealth and contribute to a better world. In short, back then we had to call for people to focus less on financial transfers; today, we have to remind people not to forget about them entirely.

We have more challenges and more means to respond to them than 70 years ago,[10] but the "aid" mentality doesn't reflect this new reality and seems stuck in the era of colonialism. If wealthy countries slowly cut their aid budgets, as conventional aid theory suggests they should, how are we planning to fight continued poverty, inequality, environmental degradation, global health crises and climate change? Can private money save the day? Can billionaires and their mega-foundations? Can brilliant charities like Oxfam? Not likely. And not desirable. While there is no denying the importance of private philanthropy, few would argue that it could or should take the place of public spending on public goods. Public goods are going to require public money. We need to overhaul our approach to international public money, expanding our ambition for it, incorporating the many new countries now helping to finance global progress, and ditching the outdated language of "aid" that many see as patronising and harmful, especially the people and governments of the Global South who resent being seen as recipients of charity rather than partners in change. In short, we need to update a tired 20th century "foreign aid" approach and, by doing so, defend internationalist ideals for the 21st century.

A new proposal

In this book I propose a new way to think about, talk about and manage the money spent by governments to support global development objectives. This new approach, which I call **Global Public Investment**, builds on the best of the traditional understanding of aid, as well as the main critiques of it, and responds to the new global reality we all face. I suggest *five major paradigm shifts* to underpin the next 50 years of financial development cooperation.

The first paradigm shift relates to the **AMBITION** of development cooperation. Foreign aid has been primarily intended to reduce poverty, both individual and the poverty of whole countries. But this focus, while important, has led to an incredibly stingy understanding of human obligations, as if the job of international solidarity is done when minimum (very low) welfare standards are met. The challenge of eradicating extreme poverty remains, but today tackling inequality and enabling all countries to converge with relatively high living standards is a bolder aim, in line with the world's new global objectives, the Sustainable Development Goals (SDGs). Furthermore, global and regional public goods are moving centre-stage, especially with the call for a Global Green New Deal[11] to combat climate chaos and ecosystem destruction, and the realisation that we need an internationalist approach to public health, both of which will require vast sums of money to achieve. Our proposal for **Global Public Investment** reflects these bolder long-term ambitions, which we will discuss in Chapter 3.

Fine, so we need to find more money. But won't private money do? And can't poorer countries pay with their own tax take? And can't billionaires help out with their philanthropy? In Chapter 4, we will look more deeply into what makes the "global" and the "public" in **Global Public Investment** so important. What is its special **FUNCTION** in responding to the challenges described in Chapter 3? Foreign aid has traditionally been considered nothing more than a stop-gap, necessary only in exceptional circumstances to fill a gap in a country's finances; as other types of finance become available, this temporary support comes to an end. But public finance has a unique set of characteristics, at the international as well as the national level, which mean it cannot simply be replaced by private, domestic or philanthropic funds.

Even when other funds come on stream, a system of **Global Public Investment** is still often the best type of finance for some interventions, not a last resort, but a first thought, prodding societies in the right direction and promoting global benefits. In other words, it is not just the quantity of a particular type of money that matters, but its unique qualities as well. Importantly, this special kind of money can play a role in all country types, not just the poorest, as well as help deal with cross-border challenges.

When it comes to the **GEOGRAPHY** of development cooperation the paradigm shift is already well underway. Changes in global wealth and power have shaken up international development practice for the better, with emerging economies now contributing more than ever to global objectives, even as they continue to receive financial support. This makes no sense in the current "aid" paradigm which splits the world into rich countries – "donors" – and poor countries – "recipients" – but is a fundamental element of the new approach we propose. In Chapter 5, I argue that all countries, even the very poorest, should contribute funds for global sustainable development according to their ability to do so, and all, even the richest, should receive, according to their need. Some will see this as a radical idea – but it is increasingly the new normal. The **Global Public Investment** proposal is not only a call to action, it is also simply a better description of today's reality.

This links closely to the fourth paradigm shift, on **GOVERNANCE**. While aid has often been a force for good, it has also been misused and wasted, in part due to the institutions and processes through which it is managed. Aid governance is stuck in the 20th century, with a handful of countries taking the major decisions and contributions fluctuating depending on "donor" circumstances. In Chapter 6 we argue that, at this time of flux, there is a moment of opportunity to reorder the way the world manages development cooperation. An improved system of **Global Public Investment** requires more democratic decision-making about the size, purpose and accountability of contributions, moving away from a donor/recipient mentality and towards more horizontal partnerships with all countries and other stakeholders (including civil society) sat at the decision-making table. There is no easy answer to the problem of global governance – power is power – but, if we get it right, **Global Public Investment** could push new types of partnership which will be the difference between an era of global progress and one in which we are unable to curtail the constant jostling of nation states for supremacy, to the detriment of marginalised communities and our planet as a whole.

The final paradigm shift is in how we talk about development cooperation. Words matter. They can convey respect or condescension – and too often in the world of "aid" it is the latter. The commonly used language of the aid sector is outdated, misleading the public, patronising recipients and entrenching an embarrassing saviour complex. A new vision for **Global Public Investment** must be accompanied by a **NARRATIVE** more appropriate to today's reality. In Chapter 7 we argue that spending on global goods and services is not a question of charity, but of sensible investment in mutually beneficial objectives (just like public sector spending at the national level). It should be an obligation, not a voluntary gift, and while it should expect a return, that return is not a financial one, but rather social and environmental impact for our global common good.

So that's the proposal. In Chapter 8 we take a step back to survey this broader landscape and discuss how the system as a whole needs to be re-purposed and better managed with the common good in mind. The shifts in approach we propose for concessional finance can also be applied to other areas of international cooperation. And we close with a call for a new era of internationalism. The concept of sending money to far-flung places without even the assurance that it will achieve its objectives is proving a hard one for many politicians and their constituents to fathom. So a major transformation in our horizons is needed if we are to respond to our common 21st century challenges: from foreign to global. This new concept of **Global Public Investment** could lead to a better, more modern, more respectful narrative around international development and cooperation. Rather than continuing the old myth of charity, we could start to use the more powerful language of solidarity, partnership, investment and mutual benefit. And rather than seeing global problems as foreign, "over there", we could make further strides forward in our understanding of our one common home – the Earth. Not Mars.

To get us going, though, one of the best ways to understand the basic idea behind **Global Public Investment** is by way of an analogy, and that is what we present in the next chapter (Chapter 2). Just as we have public spending at the national level, and at the regional level (particularly in Europe), so we need to continue to build up international public spending and investment at the global level too. These three levels are very different, but there are important similarities, which is why it is an *analogy*.

Definitions

Before we go any further we need to get some definitions out of the way. What do we mean by "aid"? How is it different from "international public finance"? And why, in the middle of what is already a very rich jargon soup, are we suggesting a whole new term: **Global Public Investment**?

"Aid" is familiar word to most people, but it is actually quite a hard concept to pin down. It is sometimes used synonymously with Official Development Assistance (ODA), the grants and low-interest loans that rich country governments make available for international development. But money raised and spent by charities (like Christian *Aid*) and major foundations (like the Gates Foundation) is usually described as "aid" too, despite not being raised by governments. Money supplied to wealthy countries is also described as "aid" (for example, when Greece received money to bail it out of financial crisis). And then there is "military *aid*" which certainly doesn't count as ODA because it doesn't focus on human welfare and economic development.[12] So "aid" is not a clearly definable pot of money and the word turns out to be quite malleable. Actually, I see it more as a mentality, an approach to spending money.

In contrast, IPF is a precise term which refers to finance raised publicly, either from national public revenue (e.g. income tax) or internationally raised levies (e.g. airline ticket tax), which is spent in another country or on some kind of cross-border project.[13] Some of it is used to support global development, as conventionally understood, but it can also be used for other purposes, such as military spending (e.g. when one country wants to help another win a war), collaboration on scientific progress (e.g. space exploration), cultural and religious projects (e.g. building churches and mosques) and export credits that have international commerce as their primary aim. Not all IPF is "concessional". Far from it. Concessional is another vague term used regularly in the world of international development finance but whose meaning is slippery. It basically means either free money (i.e. grants) or cheap money (i.e. loans at well below the market rate). *Non*-concessional finance seeks a market rate of return on investments or other benefits, such as exceptional access to an economic asset (like oil or minerals), and plenty of IPF falls into that category (think sovereign wealth funds, export credits, etc.). The thinking behind **Global Public Investment** can apply to both concessional and non-concessional spending, and as we renew our system we need to reform all types of global public finance, but the focus of this book is concessional public spending for global public goods and services, because we are concerned with two main things: a fairer distribution of wealth across the world, and a fairer system of paying for international goods and services that everyone benefits from. Concessional funds are also under the most threat, for obvious reasons, and need most political support.

This book, then, is about a certain subset of IPF that is used for the purposes of international development, sustainability and global solidarity, and is concessional. While there are already many overlapping and confusing terms in development finance there is currently no single, simple, term to describe this crucial subset of the development finance mix. That is why we need a new term: **Global Public Investment**, or **GPI**. This category is broad enough to include both ODA and South-South Cooperation (SSC) because it is not confined by OECD-managed definitions of recipients, donors, levels of concessionality and intended use. This helps to bridge a growing and unhelpful divide, without undermining the extra responsibilities of wealthy nations – the **Global Public Investment** approach doesn't undermine the need for continued redistribution and reparation, it underpins it.

The time is now

Until Covid-19, 2020 seemed to many like an odd time to be publishing a book calling for more internationalism. Political trends across the world appeared ever more nationally minded, with politicians and publics seemingly more interested in challenging and even breaking up the international order than cementing it. My country first; my country right or wrong; make my country great (again)! Multilateralism was, by most accounts, in crisis. And even those desperately fighting a rear-guard defence of international cooperation and diplomacy tended to believe that the heady days of global cooperation writ large were behind us and that a much less ambitious era of *realpolitik* had arrived. Was this really the right time to be making a bold case for much *more* internationalism, just when the limited internationalist architecture we already have seemed under such threat?

But then the virus hit, and people's perspectives began to shift radically. Covid-19 has made the deficiencies in global cooperation much more visible to many more people, and it could change – enormously, in a generational opportunity – the context within which we campaign. Policies that until recently seemed radical are now considered not only realistic but necessary. For example, with many governments now effectively paying people to stay at home and do nothing, discussion of a Universal Basic Income has reached a new level. The Spanish government is not only talking about Universal Basic Income, it has set out concrete plans to introduce it.[14] As systemic deficiencies are spotlighted in different contexts across the world, if your policy proposals in this Covid-19 moment are not radical and ambitious, you are missing the opportunity the crisis presents.

And let's not forget that while some very important parts of the international firmament are pulling back from an internationalist approach and playing an increasingly populist and nationalist hand, the Sustainable Development Goals are a clear set of instructions given by the countries of the world to themselves. The acclamation of this ambitious new set of global goals in September 2015 is one of the few pieces of good news for multilateralism and progressive internationalism of the last decade or so. They are a sign that powerful internationalist messaging is making progress all around the world, just as there are countervailing pressures that pick up most of the news headlines. At the same time calls for a Global Green New Deal to combat climate change, restore the planet and build fairer societies are gaining momentum.

The urgency of the task ahead means there is no time to waste. A major programme of international public spending is required if we are to get anywhere close to achieving social and economic development while safeguarding ecosystems and keeping well under a 1.5 degrees climate shift.[15] **Global Public Investment** is only one part of the answer to our modern global challenges – history has shown that international interventions of this kind can only accompany and complement more profound structural change at the national level. But it is a critical piece of the jigsaw.

The current moment is an opportunity to achieve something big: a more structured form of international public financing for global goods including healthcare systems and pandemic response. After all, Covid-19 already affects almost all the world's countries and regions and will not be overcome unless countries learn once again to work together, as they have done at key moments in the past. Perhaps most impressively, the Second World War induced a commitment to international monetary and trade cooperation that formed the backbone to the Bretton Woods international system. For all its weaknesses, that system was sufficient to manage the post-war rebuilding of the world. Today, a *fiscal* counterpart is required. Rather than rely on *ad hoc*, voluntary offers of financial support, couched in the language of generosity but subject to the whims of presidents and bilateral (read geopolitical) preferences, **Global Public Investment** would represent a statutory, contributory system which could be relied upon in normal times to build up health systems across the world, and in extraordinary emergencies to coordinate and finance an adequate global response.

When Keynes and others put together the pieces of a new world order after the Second World War, culminating in the Bretton Woods institutions, their ambition, clarity and strategic nous overcame the inevitable political barriers. They did what was necessary in the face of great global challenges. We are at a similar moment today. We cannot limit our vision to fit 5-year strategy periods or electoral cycles, or what seem to be the current political constraints, which can anyway change in an instant, as we have seen only too clearly in recent years. The fact that nationalist ideologies hold sway in some parts of the world means that internationalists need to fight ever harder for their ideas and ideals. Rather than self-censor to fit more neatly with what is perceived to be a popular (and populist) reaction against globalism, we need to make more persuasive arguments, based on evidence, and touching people's hearts as well as their minds. We must set out a realistic vision for this era, and work strategically to bring it to fruition. There has never been a better moment to stress the importance of internationalism and global cooperation for just and sustainable progress. This book is intended to encourage us all to be bold in our ambition, and to build new ways of thinking and doing internationally for a new century.

Notes

1. https://www.theguardian.com/global-development/2013/aug/08/aid-africa-development-bank-donald-kaberuka?CMP=twt_gu.
2. https://obamawhitehouse.archives.gov/realitycheck/the-press-office/remarks-president-clinton-global-initiative.
3. Conversation with Andy Sumner on IDS website: http://www.mixcloud.com/ids/paul-collier-and-andy-sumner-in-discussion-on-the-ids-paper-the-new-bottom-billion/.
4. https://www.gov.uk/government/speeches/justine-greening-update-on-aid-to-india. She gave a talk the following year entitled "Global trade can help us end the need for aid", see https://www.gov.uk/government/speeches/justinegreening-global-trade-can-help-us-end-the-need-for-aid.
5. https://www.livemint.com/news/india/india-facing-severe-levels-of-malnutrition-climate-change-to-further-worsen-undernutrition-11571207482952.html.
6. https://www.telegraph.co.uk/news/politics/10122842/Some-countries-do-not-need-our-money-any-more-says-Andrew-Mitchell.html.
7. World Development Indicators, World Bank.
8. Glennie (2008) The Trouble with Aid: Why less could mean more for Africa. Zed Books, London
9. https://www.cgdev.org/commitment-development-index-2018.
10. Severino and Ray (2009) described a "triple revolution" in the objectives, actors and tools used for international cooperation. Severino Jean-Michel and Ray Olivier: The End of ODA: Death and Rebirth of a Global Public Policy (2009), Center for Global Development: http://www.cgdev.org/sites/default/files/1421419_file_End_of_ODA_FINAL.pdf.

11. See for instance Pettifor (2019) The Case for the Green New Deal.
12. In 2015, the United States supplied US$5.6 billion in military aid to 63 countries. US Department of State, Foreign Military Financing Account Summary, 2015: http://www.state.gov/t/pm/ppa/sat/c14560.htm.
13. Inge Kaul, one of the few scholars that has written extensively on this subject, discusses IPF as follows: "The term 'international public finance' is frequently employed in different contexts and with different meanings. Sometimes, it denotes the transfer abroad of national public revenue for purposes like official development assistance (ODA). Other times, it may refer to international-level resource mobilization that requires a multilateral, intergovernmental approach as, for example, is necessitated by the levying of a financial transaction tax. And yet other times, it may refer to the financing of transnational – regional and global – public policy purposes, i.e. policy purposes that affect a huge range of actors, like the mitigation of global climate change, or pertain to widely shared equity concerns such as poverty reduction". https://www.ingekaul.net/wp-content/uploads/2014/01/International_Public_Financ_Fin.pdf.
14. https://www.thelocal.es/20200523/coronavirus-spain-announces-3-billion-universal-basic-income-scheme.
15. UNCTAD (2019) Trade and Development Report 2019: Financing a Global Green New Deal.

2 Scaling up
National > Regional > Global

This book will make some major proposals for rethinking aid and international public finance, outlining paradigm shifts on five main themes: Ambition, Function, Geography, Governance and Narrative. But before we look at each of these in turn, let's start with an analogy. The approach we are proposing for public spending at the global level is similar to what is already the norm at the national level in almost all countries, and at the regional level in some regions (most obviously Europe with its European Union [EU]). While it is seldom applied globally, it is an approach readers will already be quite familiar with. The mechanisms that govern national and regional public finance cannot simply be scaled up, as there are important aspects that are not replicable at the global level, but the analogy holds important clues to the transformation we have in mind.

National contributions

The importance of public spending and investment is well understood by the general public when it comes to their own countries, counties or cities. We are used to it. We don't call it aid, or charity, or use techy words like finance – we just call it public spending, the national health service, the local council. We pay our taxes, willingly or grumpily, and we expect them to contribute to a better society, whether in our own immediate neighbourhood, or in the country at large. Our money pays for parks and museums, for health and education, for transport and infrastructure, for benefits when we are out of work, disabled, old or just struggling, for security, whether police fighting crime or armies defending our borders, for subsidies to economic sectors we particularly care about (like farming), for the workforce dedicated to all of the above – nurses, teachers, rubbish collectors, civil servants.

Public spending is often painted as a political battleground between left and right, but in reality the crucial role of public spending in national economies is only criticised by the maddest tea party hatters. Sure, the left might be more open about their support for public spending, but the right are just as keen on it; for example, despite using the rhetoric of "a smaller state", the administrations of Ronald Reagan and Margaret Thatcher in the 1980s left power with a *larger* proportion of public spending then when they came to office. There is near-consensus among academics, politicians and the general public, about the importance of fairly high levels of public spending, with battles between political parties taking place around the margins of a broadly agreed framework. In most rich countries, public spending hovers at between a third and a half of annual spending. In poorer countries the proportion is generally far less although it varies widely – everyone agrees it needs to be much more.

So we are all used to public spending at the national level, and we all know why it is important. While private spending is primarily interested in benefiting the spender, whether individuals or companies, public spending is supposed to benefit society as a whole. Public spending can be counter-cyclical i.e. you can turn it up just when private spending is in decline as the business cycle turns, and public spending can have different, often longer, time horizons, whereas private capital often wants a quick buck. So public money is sometimes available when private money is not, and vice versa. Public money has a different risk profile to private money – both analyse risk and return, but differently, making them useful sources of funds for different activities. Public and private finance are two sides of a coin, with different but complementary tasks in a modern economy. Private money can, of course, be cajoled into serving public priorities when national governments take an active interest in managing private activity through measures to reduce risk, share risk and increase investment reward. But, in general, private finance does a poor job at financing public goods – that is where public spending comes into its own. Public money is accountable to the public, to voters and taxpayers, whereas private money is accountable to shareholders. And this last difference also marks public money out from charitable foundations, which are growing in importance as ever more millionaires and billionaires emerge. While these foundations often have noble objectives, in the end they are run by a few wealthy individuals and are subject to their instincts and preferences, in contrast to public money that is answerable to the people as a whole, the public.

Public spending is especially important for those on lower incomes, who may not have the capacity to pay for everything they need – it thus plays an important role in making societies more equal, which benefits both rich and poor alike. For instance, while wealthy people may have private gardens in which to spend leisure time, poorer families might go to a public park which requires public money to maintain. A richer family might be able to travel in a private car, while a poorer one relies on public transport. In most countries, people understand that taxes are needed for public spending and wealthier people are happy to invest significant amounts in public goods, even if they do not use them very often. Most people agree that some element of redistribution is sensible for reasons of fairness and societal cohesion. It also makes economic sense: an educated and healthy population enhances productivity and can create more inclusive societies, in addition to helping people realise their potential. In other words, it's a good investment. The major difference between left and right is that the left emphasises public spending on social services such as health, education and welfare, while the right often prefers military and security spending.

While public spending is sometimes couched in negative terms (i.e. making up for imperfect markets, covering areas where private financing is either impossible, undesirable or insufficient), a growing number of economists describe it in a more positive light. Mariana Mazzucato, in particular, has criticised the "market-failure" theory of state spending, arguing instead that the state has a role in "creating and shaping new markets" rather than just fixing them.[1] In particular, she has emphasised the critical role the public sector plays in financing innovation and technological change, including the internet and smartphones. For her, the public sector is an "investor of first resort",[2] which will finance the structural transformations needed to drive our economies towards net zero carbon emissions.

As you may have guessed by now, this book will be suggesting that the ways we think about public spending at the national level are appropriate as well for spending at the global level, a vastly bigger canvas, with many additional challenges, but with many similarities and lessons to learn.

One final point. Nowadays, it is accepted that a fairly large amount of public spending is needed in any well-functioning state or locality to provide public goods, things that wouldn't be available if we were all just left to our own devices. But that wasn't always the case. In fact, what seems normal now would once have been considered

outrageous. Until the 19th century, public spending in Western economies was responsible for little more than the army – it was only in
the 20th century that social and economic issues became core to its
purpose, with tax take and public spend rising steadily from fairly
low levels in most Western countries before the two world wars to
between 30% and 40% of GDP today. In Britain, for example, public
spending grew from about 18% of GDP in 1900 to over 40% today. The
transformation of the public sector into a major part of the national
economy is therefore a relatively recent 20th century phenomenon.
And it was not a foregone conclusion. It was the result of struggle and
campaigning for more equal and secure societies, where the profits of
growth were shared more fairly. Another relatively recent evolution in
public spending, and an immensely important one, is regional public
spending.

Regional contributions[3]

If the concept of public spending for the public good is by now standard at the national level, it is also increasingly well-established at the
regional level. Recent years have seen increasing regional integration,
politically and economically, across the world, and this often involves
joint public spending initiatives. The African Union's Peace Fund, for
instance, pools money from the countries of Africa to spend on medi-
ation, institutional capacity and peace support.[4] And Africa Centres
for Disease Control and Prevention have grown in prominence since
the coronavirus outbreak – one of many regionally funded initiatives.
The regional development banks are examples of countries pooling
money to support their joint and several needs in a particular region,
both within national borders and cross-border challenges requiring
joint-working. The Asian Development Bank's ASEAN Infrastructure
Fund, to take just one of many examples, pools money from the Bank's
members to invest in transport, energy and other projects, with a particular focus on the greening of infrastructure.[5] The EU is the world's
most ambitious and bureaucratically complex regional grouping – it
is the only regional grouping that jointly negotiates trade deals, for
example, and seeks some kind of joint foreign policy. Importantly, for
this analogy, it has been a pioneer in regional public spending and
investment. So let's look at it in a bit more detail.

The vision at the heart of the EU's "structural and investment funds"
is not just poverty reduction, but convergence to a common standard,
"narrow[ing] the development disparities among regions and member
states".[6] Through these funds, the EU has spent decades redistributing

billions of Euros every year between its members. The three main funds are the European Regional Development Fund (ERDF), the European Social Fund (ESF) and the Cohesion Fund (CF) – these funds were allocated a total of €351.8 billion for the 2014–20 period, 32.5% of the EU's overall budget.[7] The money has been spent on infrastructure development, job creation, small business development and entrepreneurship, research and innovation and environmental protection. As well as closing economic and social disparities, the funds also focus on greater connectivity between European countries, such as cross-European transport networks.[8] Two further funds – the European Agricultural Fund for Rural Development (EAFRD) and the European Maritime and Fisheries Fund (EMFF) – target rural and maritime sectors with an additional €91.5 billion. Another fund, the EU Solidarity Fund, has provided emergency financing totalling over €5 billion to 24 different European countries in response to over 80 disasters including floods, forest fires, earthquakes, storms and drought.[9] All these funds provide most of their assistance in the form of non-repayable grants, although loans, interest-rate subsidies, guarantees and equity are also sometimes used.

How important are these funds for the EU's members? For some, they have been hugely important. For example, in the 1990s, Spain absorbed more than 20% of the EU's structural and cohesion funding, which helped build the country's transport infrastructure.[10] As recently as 2018 it was still a net recipient of EU funds – it paid in €10.3 billion and received back €12.3 billion (about 1% of the Spanish economy), a net gain of €2 billion.[11] According to former Spanish Secretary of State for European Affairs, Diego López Garrido, "We joined the European Union when our income was around 75% of the European average, and we are now above that average. This would not have happened without a policy of European solidarity, expressed by the structural funds".[12]

Ireland is another poster child for the success of EU funds in boosting growth and convergence. Between 1987 and 2000, Ireland's economy expanded by 140%, moving from about 70% of the EU average, to about 110%. This coincided with a large increase in receipts from EU funds from 1989 onwards. While it's hard to isolate the impact of the EU funds from other factors which contributed to this impressive economic performance (such as access to the EU single market), evaluations of the EU's funds in Ireland suggest that the amount of cash that was injected into the Irish economy in the 1990s – at one point up to 4% of Irish GDP – was large enough to have had an overall positive economic impact. Ireland used this money to invest in human resources, education and training, a key factor in making Ireland an attractive destination for foreign direct investment.[13]

Since 2000, it has been the countries of Eastern Europe that have most benefited. When 10 post-communist countries joined the EU in 2004, their per capita incomes were a fraction of that of the 15 older member states. But with EU accession came access to billions in intra-regional development funding. Take Poland, the largest of this group. It received about €10 billion a year in development funds between 2007 and 13,[14] roughly 3% of its GDP. Over this period, the country experienced a 65% increase in its per capita income to become the world's 49th richest country by that measurement. Despite this growing wealth, the EU set aside a further €60 billion for Poland over the 2014–20 period,[15] with the aim of continuing to support investment in roads, hospitals, schools and other infrastructure needed to "narrow the development disparity" with other EU countries.

Importantly, it is not only the poorer countries in the EU which benefit, but also the less advantaged regions within wealthier members. For instance, the European Regional Development Fund allocated €11 billion to Germany, the EU's wealthiest country, in the 2014–2020 budget.[16] This money was used to promote social cohesion, generate jobs and invest in green growth.

Overall, in the period 2007–13, the EU says its funds helped increase income in the poorest EU regions, support 2.4 million people to find a job, support 198,000 small and medium-sized enterprises (SMEs) with direct investment (including 77,800 start-ups), support 61,000 research projects, increase broadband connectivity for 5 million EU citizens, modernise water supply systems, support 9,400 projects to improve the sustainability and attractiveness of towns and cities, and build 1,200 km of roads and 1,500 km of railway line.[17] Not bad. You don't necessarily have to believe all the claims made by the EU for the impact of this money (some of this spending will, no doubt, have been poorly used) to see the many lessons that can be learned from the European experience for public investment in other regions and at the global level. In fact, in some ways it embodies the five paradigm shifts proposed in this book.

Take AMBITION. Clearly, concessional public finance from abroad can do a lot more than respond to the worst effects of extreme poverty. In the case of the EU it plays a redistributive role, responding to poverty and inequality within the region and supporting the convergence of living standards, while helping build regional public goods, particularly infrastructure and communications. Its FUNCTION goes well beyond just filling gaps, as is clear from the fact that relatively wealthy countries benefit from it, while being very far from dependent on it. In fact, the evidence indicates that it is even more effective in more advanced, less dependent countries, where institutions tend to be more solid. While all the talk in the "aid" sector internationally is of the inevitable shift from grants to loans as countries grow economically, the EU example shows that countries well up the income scale can benefit from grants and don't need to "graduate" to loans. Regarding GEOGRAPHY, although some countries are net contributors and others net recipients, all countries in the Union benefit in different ways. Rather than talk of donors and recipients, whereby some countries give and others receive, this is a membership model whereby all contribute and all receive. This has implications for GOVERNANCE – because all countries pay in, even if they are net recipients, all are at the table at regular meetings where decisions are made about policy and budgets. The EU puts the recipients of funds themselves in the driving seat, recognising that it is national and local governments that are best-placed to decide how funds should be used. And, finally, the NARRATIVE is not of charity and generosity received gratefully by needy beneficiaries, but of partnership in a common endeavour.

Critical to the theory underpinning the EU funds, and to garnering public support for this large-scale redistribution of wealth, is the realisation that reducing disparities in living standards and building shared infrastructure is important for the progress of all, not just the direct recipients of grants. Net-contributor countries have benefited from having healthier and wealthier neighbours, which can participate more actively in trade. And the companies of net-contributor countries can also participate in EU-funded projects – German companies, for instance, helped to deliver Spain's infrastructure. Mutual benefit is at the heart of the model, as the countries of the EU seek to build a more secure and prosperous region in which to thrive.

From national/regional to global

The concepts with which we are all familiar when it comes to public spending in cities, counties, countries and regions can be usefully applied to global public spending as well. But it means shifting our starting point well away from the traditional "foreign aid" approach. At the national and regional levels we practice redistribution, but we don't describe it as charity. We are concerned with poverty, but not limited by an exclusive poverty focus. We target sub-national geographies (e.g. disadvantaged towns and counties) not just countries. We manage our money democratically, with net recipients as well as net contributors sat around the decision-making table. Crucially, we don't expect national and regional public spending to gradually reduce – if anything, we want to continue to increase it over time. We are onto something good, a successful direction that human society has adopted in the 20th century and one to build on in the 21st, as its powerful impact is demonstrated ever more clearly. National and regional public spending has not been an unfortunate but necessary blip until private money takes over – in fact in many parts of the world it is still in its infancy. It is growing and it is here to stay. Just as citizens accept the concept of taxation to pay for national public goods, and just as many countries accept the need to contribute to cohesive regions, so we need to develop language to make that the new normal at a global level. And that means a new way of thinking, which establishes concessional IPF as a permanent part of the fabric of our world: **Global Public Investment**.

Public investment implemented at a global scale would work very differently. Most crucially, perhaps, the governance and accountability arrangements that work in most countries or in cohesive regions like Europe do not exist at a global scale, meaning that money would need to be managed quite differently. The analogy looks at certain aspects of the national and EU models and should not be taken for an endorsement of all aspects of those models. We are not suggesting something like the EU model writ large on a global scale. Importantly, in the national and European regional examples, money is collected into a central budget and then distributed by central committees – nothing of the kind is desirable or plausible at a global scale, where it is much more likely that, as now, a thousand flowers would bloom when it comes to governance. And it is worth noting, as one of the largest EU countries (the UK) has recently voted to leave the EU, that you could perfectly well have voted for Brexit but still see the value of the EU funds.

Instead, this analogy gives the broad brushstrokes of what a different approach might look like, an approach that is already emerging in many contexts, including the rise of climate finance, which follows a different narrative and already accommodates some of the paradigm shifts set out in this book. Some of the major global and regional funds (such as the Global Fund to Fight AIDS, Tuberculosis and Malaria, known as the Global Fund) are pioneering new funding, governance and spending models along the lines set out here, as are some of the regional and thematic development banks.

The analogy is particularly useful in prompting questions about why some of the concepts regularly used at the national and regional levels have generally not been applied to global concerns. Does it point to some kind of contradiction, even hypocrisy, about the way wealthy countries treat people and countries in the Global South? For instance, it is clear EU policy and practice, as voted by EU member states, that continued redistribution to countries high up the income per capita scale represents a good use of taxpayers' money (all EU members except Hungary and Romania are considered "high-income") and indeed the evidence implies that it could be transformational. Why, then, do these same EU members argue that "aid" money should be reduced, and eventually axed, in parts of the world which need social sector and infrastructural support much more urgently? The EU has announced plans to withdraw its aid from many so-called "middle-income" countries,[18] like South Africa, Vietnam and Indonesia, and the bilateral programmes of EU member states are heading in the same direction, arguing that these countries are "now in a position to fund [their] own development".[19] Vietnam's GDP per capita is about US$2,500 (in Poland it is over US$15,000) and it is home to almost 30 million people whose basic needs are not being met.[20] Hungary and Romania, Ireland and Spain have not "graduated from aid" because EU funding is not limited to a poverty-focus but is concerned also with growth, infrastructure and convergence with higher living standards in neighbouring countries. Why should that goal be appropriate for members of the EU and not for all countries? It is for the reader to contemplate that question. Might it be that the aid mentality, which matured in the era of colonialism and post-colonialism, has different expectations for European countries than for other countries in the world? Might it be that what is considered acceptable in poorer countries in the Global South would never be considered acceptable in the European gang?

Rather than reducing grants to poorer countries elsewhere in the world, the EU should be increasing them, just as they have done closer to home. And rather than just organising a huge post-covid stimulus package for the relatively wealthy countries of Europe, a similarly drastic intervention is required across the world.[21] With the adoption of the SDGs, and in the time of Covid-19, the door for applying EU-style thinking to a broader global context seems to be wide open, not just post-2030, but post-2050 and beyond. If proposing a new permanent status for concessional international public finance sounds radical, remember that support for national and regional level public finance needed to be built over decades and is still in the process of construction. The same gradual process of legitimisation could be on the way for **Global Public Investment**, especially given the scale of the challenges facing our globe, which is the subject to which we now turn.

Notes

1. http://www.sussex.ac.uk/spru/newsandevents/2014h/conferences/mofi.
2. https://www.nytimes.com/2019/11/26/business/mariana-mazzucato.html.
3. Some of these reflections were first made in an article for the Guardian which I wrote with Gail Hurley (2014).
4. https://au.int/en/aureforms/peacefund.
5. https://www.adb.org/site/funds/funds/asean-infrastructure-fund.
6. https://ec.europa.eu/regional_policy/en/information/publications/legislation/2015/european-structural-and-investment-funds-2014-2020-official-texts-and-commentaries.
7. https://eur-lex.europa.eu/summary/glossary/structural_cohesion_fund.html?locale=en.
8. https://ec.europa.eu/regional_policy/sources/docgener/informat/basic/basic_2014_en.pdf.
9. See: https://ec.europa.eu/regional_policy/en/funding/solidarity-fund/.
10. https://www.theguardian.com/commentisfree/2014/may/01/eu-poland-10-years-economic.
11. https://europa.eu/european-union/about-eu/countries/member-countries/spain_en.
12. Source: http://www.openeurope.org.uk/Content/Documents/Pdfs/2012EU-structuralfunds.pdf.
13. http://www.iro.ie/EU-structural-funds.html.
14. https://www.paih.gov.pl/europeanfunds.
15. https://www.theguardian.com/commentisfree/2014/may/01/eu-poland-10-years-economic.
16. https://www.dw.com/en/how-the-eu-funds-its-economically-disadvantaged-regions/a-48354538.
17. Success Stories: Growth and Jobs Created Through the EU Budget: https://www.europarl.europa.eu/RegData/etudes/IDAN/2014/490693/IPOL_IDA(2014)490693_EN.pdf.
18. https://www.odi.org/sites/odi.org.uk/files/odi-assets/publications-opinion-files/8382.pdf.
19. https://www.gov.uk/government/news/uk-to-end-direct-financial-support-to-south-africa.
20. Using the $5.50 poverty line of the World Bank, WDI.
21. https://edition.cnn.com/2020/04/10/business/europe-coronavirus-stimulus/index.html.

3 AMBITION
From survive to thrive

> • *Traditional analysis*: **Foreign aid** is intended to reduce poverty, and it should cease when an agreed minimum threshold of development is reached. The end is in sight.
>
> • *New paradigm*: **Global Public Investment** should promote sustainability, equality and global prosperity, as well as target poverty. This is a long-term project.

After bubbling under the surface for four decades, the concept of sustainable development, which links social, economic and environmental concerns, has finally been adopted as the basis for international cooperation. While non-binding, the Sustainable Development Goals are the international community's most significant "to-do list", and they are vastly more ambitious than their predecessors, the Millennium Development Goals, widening the scope of international cooperation almost exponentially. Their new transformational vision encourages governments to take collective action to tackle inequality, address climate change, protect the environment, support innovation, drive new technologies and promote peace and prosperity everywhere.[1] In this chapter, we look at how the AMBITION of the international community needs to continue to evolve – our first paradigm shift.

Coronavirus changes the game

In December 2019 cases of a new disease were reported in Wuhan, a Chinese city with a population of about 11 million. Eleven months later (as this book goes to press), hundreds of thousands of people are confirmed dead worldwide. Countries all over the world have endured long periods of lockdown in attempts to quell the global pandemic.

If ever proof were needed that health concerns arising in one country require a coordinated and well-funded global response, this is it.

Just as public money is required within the borders of each country, an effective pandemic response will require very large sums of public money at the international level. As usual when we look beyond our own town and city limits, our national borders, the reasons to engage in joint solutions are a combination of self-interest and solidarity. Self-interest because the Covid-19 virus is attacking everyone, no matter where they live in the world, rich or poor. It is, in that sense, a great equaliser (it has also framed the great inequalities that characterise our modern world). Even if one country manages to get on top of it in the short to medium term, there is no way back to normality without most other countries doing the same. In a globalised world, where intercontinental travel can be quicker than getting around your own country, it's not just our immediate neighbours that we need to worry about – it's the whole planet. And solidarity because, in any case, could people in some countries simply watch while Covid-19 tears other countries apart and kills thousands of people, simply because they happen to be in regions less fortunate than their own? Hopefully, we have not reached such a breakdown of humanity and empathy.

This global ramping up of public spending would support three goals: to respond to the immediate urgency of producing and distributing the protective equipment, test kits and treatment options needed at scale in all affected countries; to invest in and fast-track the production of affordable and effective new drugs as well as a vaccine manufactured and distributed at scale and at pace; and to support poorer countries as they face unprecedented demands on their balance sheets, both in the immediate term, and in the aftermath of the crisis. Huge challenges are always beaten through strong international cooperation – bringing together the vast intellectual, technological and financial resources available in our global village. Multilateralism is under the spotlight and some of today's avowedly nationalist political leaders may eschew the opportunity to work together. But we can't allow the best ideas to be held back – those willing to engage should do so, and hope that others will join as they see the impact of solidarity in action. Covid-19 may be the pandemic that showed us that global solidarity is not just a nice idea – it is a necessity.

The fact that one man, Bill Gates, is the World Health Organisation's (WHO) second largest funder tells you all you need to know about the global community's commitment to the organisation. It cannot operate fully or effectively without a larger and more independently financed core budget. Clearly we need some sort of short-term, emergency resolution, providing greater funds to the WHO directly in response to Covid-19. But such an urgent response does not overcome the basic problem which is the total global burden of disease and the ever-closer interconnections between unevenly equipped national and regional health systems. So we need a more sure-footed response to the current pandemic, one that will also help us to avoid the next one, to finance the likely ongoing health crisis over the longer term, especially in poorer parts of the world, and to meet the existing international aims of the SDGs.

While rich countries' development agencies tie themselves in knots over whether the money they spend in response should come from the "aid" budget, they are missing the larger picture. This is not just about transferring money from one country to another, but pooling resources to solve global problems. We are all in this together. Coronavirus is only the latest in a long line of epidemics that have affected humans all over the planet, from HIV to bird flu to Ebola, and many more. Global public goods need global public responses, financed by global public money, bringing all countries together to work on common endeavours. The "aid" mentality is holding us back. We don't have the language to explain what is happening in front of our eyes, or respond to modern challenges. We need a bigger picture understanding of concessional international public finance fit for the 21st century. It's time for a new approach.

Sustainability

But health is far from being the only global good we need to work on collectively. Until the Covid-19 crisis dominated everything, the major threat everyone talked about was climate change and the broader challenge of global environmental sustainability. The MDGs had only one goal focused on environmental issues and even this goal was something of an afterthought, according to an anecdote told by Mark Malloch-Brown, the former head of the UN Development Programme (UNDP), who claims to have added MDG7 only after a chance meeting with the head of the UN Environment Programme (UNEP) in the corridor.[2] By contrast, environmental sustainability is a thread weaving through almost all of the 17 SDGs, which include targets for sustainable agriculture, sustainable management of water and sanitation, sustainable energy, sustainable infrastructure and industrialisation, sustainable cities, sustainable consumption and production, a focus on oceans, seas and marine resources and a focus on land and forests.

Climate change, and the ensuing chaos, is probably the biggest challenge humanity has ever faced. While the UN's Inter-governmental

Panel on Climate Change (IPCC) insists that we must contain global warming to within 2C, itself a concession on the initial limit of 1.5C,[3] some scientists warn that the temperature rise could reach 3C or even 5C by the end of the century unless there are immediate radical reductions in carbon emissions.[4] And that would mean drought, floods, extreme heat, wildfires, food shortages and poverty for hundreds of millions of people. Climate change is already contributing to an increase in the frequency and severity of extreme weather events and disasters around the world. In 2017, Hurricanes Irma and Maria devastated parts of the Caribbean. In the aftermath, Gaston Browne, prime minister of Antigua and Barbuda, declared Barbuda "rubble" and "barely habitable", and implemented a mandatory evacuation order to move the island's 1,800 residents to safety. It was the first time the island had been uninhabited in over 300 years.[5] According to the world's leading scientists, whole nations may vanish over the next 50–100 years.[6] It is now 10 years since the government of the Maldives held an underwater cabinet meeting to draw attention to the climate change perils faced by low-lying atoll nations, and still change seems snail-paced.[7]

Meanwhile, degradation of unique ecosystems continues apace. Earth's species are undergoing what some experts have termed the "sixth mass extinction" due to habitat loss, poaching, pollution and climate change.[8] The number of wild animals living on Earth is falling rapidly, caused mainly by the destruction of wild areas for farming and logging with just four commodities – beef, soy, palm oil and wood – driving the majority of tropical deforestation. In the world's oceans, seas and lakes, over a third of wild fish stocks are being fished at biologically unsustainable levels, while global demand for fish continues to climb.[9] Insects are essential for the proper functioning of all ecosystems, but they are in precipitous decline with a rate of extinction eight times that of mammals, birds and reptiles; 40% of all insect species are currently threatened with extinction.[10] The Earth has lost about 70% its wetlands over the last 30 years alone, from the Caribbean coral reefs to the Alaskan kelp forest. The Aral Sea between Kazakhstan and Uzbekistan has "already collapsed" and is considered unrecoverable.[11] It is not uncommon to read headlines that state simply: "Ecosystems the size of the Amazon can collapse within decades".[12]

There is not space in a short book to list the many threats to the planet and to humanity related to our unsustainable growth model. The point is that concerted international cooperation will be required to get the Earth back on track. The need for structural transformation in poorer countries to bring extreme poverty to an end, reduce inequality and promote sustainability and the need for "green" rather than dirty growth has changed the game for international public funds. If industrialised countries are serious about asking poorer countries to keep global CO_2 emissions to a minimum, in a context where they are struggling to reduce their own emissions, they will need to pay poorer countries for this costly environmental service, a principle established in the United Nations (UN) Climate Change Conferences over the last three decades. The SDGs will require action at national, regional and global levels and represent a significant addition to the priorities of the international community – but only the response to climate change (mitigation and adaptation) has so far received significant (if inadequate) financial support.

Estimates vary as to how much it will cost to reverse climate change and ecological degradation diverge but are invariably high. The costs of *not* dealing with climate change have been well-known for a long time. Way back in 2006 the Stern Review estimated them to be equivalent to losing at least 5% of global GDP each year, possibly rising to over 20%.[13] Avoiding this damage requires transforming the world economy at a speed and scale that has "no documented historic precedent", according to the authors of the IPCC's 2018 report, who warn of up to US$54 trillion worth of damage.[14] Some *ad hoc* schemes do exist to provide compensation to governments, landowners or communities for maintaining or improving natural ecosystems, but not on a systematic basis or to scale.

International development cooperation to date has tended to focus on the national level, as evidenced by the way the vast majority of ODA is spent. But we now recognise much better all the challenges that respect no national boundaries – we have looked at health and environmental issues, but there are many others. What about crime and security, from organised mafia activities to international piracy, to conflict hotspots around the world to the continued menace of sophisticated terrorism? And then there's migration, one of a number of huge topics that will be simply impossible to cover in a short book. In 2013 the UN's High Commissioner for Refugees at the time, Antonio Guterres, reported that his agency had "never had to address so much human misery in its 64-year history", with over 51 million people around the world uprooted from their homes due to conflict and persecution.[15] Turkey is currently home to more than 2.2 million Syrians and Lebanon registers an astonishing one refugee for every four inhabitants.

So the concept of international public goods and services (regional and global) is once again coming to the fore.[16] If national public finance is intended, broadly, to support national public goods, it seems natural that one of the objectives of global public finance is to support global public goods.[17] The private sector can't do it because public goods are non-exclusive i.e. everyone benefits from them, so it is impossible to make a profit by excluding some people from consumption. This clear market failure must be addressed by governments. While it might be expensive at first, part of the reason to support global public goods is the collective efficiency gains they bring: whether fighting Covid-19, global warming or crime syndicates, the international community can make more cost-effective progress if it works together.

If the provision of public goods and services at a global scale is required to create a favourable environment for domestic development efforts, the reverse is also true. We can't ensure global goods unless countries themselves are able and willing to play their part. As the provision of global public goods grows in importance, so does the need for funds to support the domestic complementary components required for their generation and utilisation. To take the health example again, there is no global health system without hundreds of well-functioning national health systems. And there is no global environmental sustainability unless every country in the world can protect its own environment. So for all the talk of global well-being, we can't get away from the need to support specific countries in their efforts to progress. And that is an area where we also need a step-change in our ambitions.

Stingy and arbitrary poverty thresholds

In order to understand the traditional (and still dominant) approach to foreign aid, we need to interrogate the idea of "poverty". In 1978 the World Bank's Managing Director, Robert McNamara, coined the term "absolute poverty" which he described as "a condition of life so characterized by malnutrition, illiteracy, disease, squalid surroundings, high infant mortality, and low life expectancy as to be beneath any reasonable definition of human decency".[18] So, is the fight against absolute poverty being won? The evidence is mixed. Some key indicators show incredible progress over the past few decades. Life expectancy in low-income countries has risen from 43 years in 1970 to nearer 63 in 2017, meaning people in the poorest parts of the world are living an average of 20 years longer. Meanwhile, the proportion of mothers dying in childbirth has almost halved since 2000 in the same countries. Sub-Saharan Africa often lags behind in these measures, but there has been crucial progress in this region too, as the infant mortality rate has reduced from 180 per 1,000 in 1990 to 78 in 2018. More girls are completing primary school than at any other time in history.[19] So don't let anyone tell you that change isn't possible.

However, celebration of progress must be tempered with clarity about how far there is to go, and concern about the possibility of regression. The latest World Bank estimate is that about half the world – almost 4 billion people – lives on under $5.50 per day, meaning they are not meeting "minimum basic needs".[20] And due to growing populations, more people were living on under $5.50 per day in 2015 than in 1990 in some regions of the world, including the Middle East and North Africa, South Asia and sub-Saharan Africa (taking into account inflation and exchange rates). This level of poverty is set to remain in most countries for the foreseeable future – or worsen, given the impact of Covid-19 and associated economic downturns, which may have set the fight against absolute poverty back at least a decade by some estimates.[21] Even if one is optimistic about reducing extreme poverty, projections for the next 20 years show a burgeoning mass of insecure people in the $2–$10 range. And that isn't yet taking into account the possibly devastating impact of climate chaos.

So looking just at poverty, there are tough times ahead for the world's poorest communities which will require enhanced global responses. But we need to go further than a tight poverty focus. The MDG era succeeded in focusing the world on the worst excesses of human poverty in a world of plenty, and ending extreme poverty rightly remains the main priority of the international community; rather than just seeking to halve income poverty, which was the MDG objective, the SDGs call for the eradication of extreme poverty by 2030.[22] But one of the consequences of this important poverty focus has been the perception that when the worst forms of deprivation are dealt with, the job of the international community is largely done.[23] This is a mistake. When families pull themselves up above the $1.90/day line, they still face terrible hardship and insecurity. Poverty "just above the line" is only marginally better, by definition, than poverty just below it. The international development community has placed too much emphasis on an arbitrary and exaggeratedly stingy definition of extreme poverty.

Since the late 1970s the World Bank has divided the world into low-, middle- and high-income countries.[24] Countries are dubbed "low-income" if their income per capita is less than US$1,025 per year. When it rises above that point they become "middle-income". The idea is that aid helps poor countries become wealthier, moving up this low/middle/high-income scale. When a country's income per capita reaches a certain level, so the thinking goes, it will no longer require aid – a process called "graduation". It's a simple logic, and it is at the heart of decision-making about aid.

And the same logic is applied to people. The aid industry uses various techniques to define human poverty, but they all coalesce around the idea that there are some basic material necessities which people require to live decent lives. A certain amount of food every day; the expectation that, in normal circumstances, mothers will survive childbirth and children will survive into adolescence; a roof over your head; a functioning toilet. Economists (mostly, again, at the World Bank) calculate a proxy for poverty by assessing household income, which is where we get "dollar-a-day" poverty measures from. On current calculations, if you earn less than $1.90 per day you are counted as "extremely poor".

In both cases, for countries and for people, "poverty" is defined in absolute terms, rather than relatively. This means it is possible that one day there will be no countries or people left in poverty, and indeed it is a favourite pastime in the aid sector to countdown the number of people still living in "poverty" and the number of countries still considered "low-income". But there are two big problems with these thresholds: they are arbitrary and stingy. Take the dollar-a-day poverty measures. According to Lant Pritchett, a member of the World Bank team that launched these measurements, they were worried about being accused of overstating poverty numbers as a way of winning more resources so they chose a poverty line so stingy no one could dispute that a person below the line was poor. So much for detailed economic analysis! The poverty line was set arbitrarily and stingily, with a view to what would fly among donor countries. Of course, maths and equations are offered in support, but, in the words of Pritchett, "All this poverty stuff is a holy mess once you dig into it. There is no real science behind any of it".[25]

The same goes for the low/middle/high-income thresholds for countries. According to the World Bank, the number of "low-income" countries has reduced from around 60 in 2000 to nearer 30 today. Until the coronavirus outbreak, some estimated that there would be fewer than 16 low-income countries by 2030, mostly in Africa.[26] The calculations underpinning these thresholds are not in the public domain, but there is no doubt that they were just as random. And they are equally stingy. More than one-third of the world's malnourished children live in India, where prevalence is double that of sub-Saharan Africa. India has been a "middle-income" country since 2007. Meanwhile South Sudan emerged onto the international scene as a "middle-income" country in 2011, despite facing some of the gravest challenges on the planet. In 2012 it became "low-income" again, as oil exports fell. Guatemala has been an "upper-middle-income" country for decades, despite having one of the highest rates of chronic malnutrition in the world, with almost 50% prevalence of stunting.[27] The words "middle-income" are themselves unhelpful in communicating development realities to busy politicians, journalists and the public at large who quite fairly assume that such countries are no longer poor, which is simply not true, certainly not by any definition of poverty that the rich world would accept. In short, people in the Global South described by these economists as "no longer poor" would be considered destitute in the Global North.

With the number of "poor" people and countries apparently reducing, traditional thinking suggests we should be preparing for the end of the aid project. Research studies are being written on how best to exit from aid intended for the many countries facing the imminent and unwelcome prospect of "graduation". But this traditional approach is misguided. These international poverty lines were intended to identify the most destitute people on the planet, not to stipulate an acceptable standard of living.[28] A subtle and self-serving sleight of hand is taking place whereby prioritisation (i.e. analysing, quite sensibly, which people and countries require *most* support) is being confused with need (i.e. going on to say that people and countries outside of this narrow band don't need support *at all*). "Need" turns out to be quite an interesting word. Do people in Europe really "need" the generous social welfare systems they enjoy, the subsidised transport, the publicly funded libraries and parks? Well, yes, most Europeans seem to think so. But then why is a thoroughly different version of "need" applied to people living in Africa, Asia or Latin America, which are apparently now ready to graduate from financial assistance despite half their children being malnourished?

To be clear, it is useful to measure levels of poverty; the problem is that these measurements are carrying a weight for which they were never intended, placing arbitrariness and stinginess at the heart of decision-making. Attempts to instigate somewhat more generous poverty lines (the World Bank now also measures $3.20 and $5.50 per day poverty) are steps in the right direction but the point remains. What happens if the world does finally eradicate "poverty" according to the various thresholds defined by World Bank economists? Does international solidarity then just pack up and go home? No. Despite what you will still hear many Western politicians and economists say, the responsibility of the international community does not end when McNamara's "absolute poverty" is dealt with, or when "basic needs" are met. That would be an absurdly low ambition, and not at all in line with SDG thinking. On the contrary, when the worst forms of poverty are ended (and we are still some way from that), the job of international cooperation, including financial redistribution, has still only just started. Adolf Kloke-Lesch, a former Managing Director at GIZ, the German development agency, summarised this succinctly: *"Development only really begins when extreme poverty is eradicated".*[29] Without losing a focus on the very poorest, the international community should live up to its obligations to the billions of people living marginally above arbitrarily defined global poverty lines. In fact, it should follow the EU's lead and aim for a general convergence of living standards across the world? This brings us to what we should now be staking out as the modern ambition of international cooperation: reducing inequality.

Global convergence

Although the aid sector defines international poverty in absolute terms, most countries define it relatively. In the UK, for example, you are considered poor if you earn under 60% of the median income (the income that half adults earn more than, and half earn less than). That means that as incomes rise the poorest citizens should expect public support to maintain higher standards of living. A society that defines poverty relatively rather than absolutely is making a very different ethical proposition, implying it is not just interested in the poorest people scraping by with the bare minimum, but in everyone living within touching distance of each other, enjoying the fruits of a country's economic progress.

This simple shift in approach could transform our ambition as an international community as well. Calculating median income worldwide is tricky, as problems like exchange rates and varying costs of living get in the way. And, anyway, it may be better to use mean rather than median income to give a real idea of inequality, or to look at wealth rather than income, to take into account this more deep-seated type of economic advantage. We can leave the details of measuring inequality for now. The fundamental point is that if we shift our analysis away from absolute poverty thresholds towards relative measures, we get a very different picture of poverty across the world. All people, and all countries, should expect the same social and economic standards that richer nations today take for granted, and the international community should work towards achieving that – just as we do at the national level.

Our global economy operates within natural limits, but our development model has jeopardised the well-being of future generations without even meeting the needs of the present. With the adoption of the SDGs, the international community has finally formally recognised the need to live within the natural boundaries of the planet, even if that recognition is not yet represented in sufficient public policy shifts. The concept of sustainable development has equality indelibly associated with it: in a world of limited resources and a growing population, sharing things out more equally in the 21st century may be the only way humanity can survive into the 22nd. British economist, Kate Raworth, has championed the idea of the "doughnut", a set of social and planetary boundaries, within which we must live and which, if breached, could lead to tipping points in key Earth systems such as ocean acidification, chemical and air pollution, biodiversity and land quality.[30]

At its heart the SDG vision is of a more equal world. Let's take the health sector. Overall, the MDG era was one of real progress: more than 80% of the world's children are now vaccinated against measles; the number of births per woman has dropped substantially and child survival rates are higher. It is not all good news by any means – most MDG targets remain unmet, we are going backwards on some indicators (such as the number of chronically undernourished, which has risen in recent years[31]) and even where progress has been made, it is often not consolidated, meaning we could see backsliding. Nevertheless, there is much to celebrate. But the SDGs take us to a whole other level. While the MDGs focused on basic health, ensuring that everyone has access to the bare minimum basic healthcare – in itself a huge and complex task – the SDGs set out ambitions for *all* levels of healthcare – primary, secondary and tertiary. While the MDGs had clear targets for three specific focus areas – child mortality (MDG4), maternal health (MDG5) and combating major diseases (MDG6) – the health SDG (SDG3) calls for good health for all people of all ages, and specifies progress on such diverse issues as non-communicable diseases, drug abuse and road accidents. This is much more than unfinished business; this is a sea-change in the ambition of the international community on social progress.[32] It has opened the door to a radically more ambitious vision for global health in the 21st century: universal health coverage, or UHC, is a concept now accepted by most governments, even if there are still definitional discussions. While it does not mean full equality of health access, an ideal that is not met in any country, it is a step down that road.

Crucially, a focus on system strengthening has finally risen to the top of the global health agenda; systems and institutions need to be in place to ensure long-term and sustained health provision. This has serious implications for the way we view international development cooperation. People across the world, including in poorer countries, rightly expect much more than containment of the direst health problems. In fact, they increasingly expect convergence with the standards of healthcare enjoyed by citizens of wealthier countries. The place you happen to have been born should not dictate the quality of your healthcare. So the fact that some Southern countries are now able to provide certain basic health services without international assistance emphatically does not mean that the job of international cooperation is done.

Let's use life expectancy to demonstrate how our proposed approach, focusing on relative living standards, differs from the traditional "aid" perspective. Average life expectancy is a good news global story, standing at just over 72 years worldwide today, compared to just under 59 in 1970. The traditional aid mentality would set a life expectancy threshold above which people are considered to live long enough lives, and reduce aid accordingly. Given that in 1970 countries like Italy had an average life expectancy of under 60, let's say that 60 would be a fair threshold. So countries that today have a life expectancy of over 60 – which is just about every country in the world, including Burkina Faso, Benin and Haiti – would no longer qualify for support. Contrastingly, an approach based on relative standards would keep shifting this threshold as life expectancy in the rest of the world rises and would work to reduce the difference between average life expectancy in different countries. Countries would require support as long as their life expectancy was significantly different to the world's top life expectancy (currently Japan, 84).

That is certainly how we think about things at the country level, so why should it be any different globally? There are parts of the UK, for instance, where people live much shorter lives than the national average, Glasgow being the most frequently cited. Life expectancy for Glaswegians at the turn of the 19th century was just over 40 years, rising to 70 in the 1980s and about 75 today. That is a huge improvement. But life expectancy in Glasgow is about 6 years below the UK national average of 81.[33] For a variety of reasons, which are the subject of much discussion, Glaswegians die sooner than most of their compatriots and the policy response, quite rightly, is to analyse the discrepancy and work to reduce it, using public policy and public finance among other tools. Woe betide a politician suggesting that because Glaswegians live longer than they did 50 or 100 years ago we need no longer worry about their relatively lower life expectancy – that would be considered callous in the extreme. And yet that is effectively the traditional aid approach. It is no less callous because it refers to people in other continents, than it would be if applied to people in the same country. That is the essence of internationalism.

And this new perspective can be applied to all sectors of society, not just health. Take education, where the SDGs signal a similar step-change in ambition: while the education MDG (2) focused only on primary education, the education SDG (4) includes secondary and even tertiary education in its scope as well. The aid approach embodied by the MDGs consistently aims low for what is expected for the world's poor people and countries – a new approach, already substantially laid out in the SDGs, should aim high.

What would all this mean in practice? First, we need to stop thinking of aid as temporary and start thinking of permanent **Global Public Investment**. While it is all but inevitable that the world will continue to push people and countries over arbitrary poverty, health, education and other thresholds, the challenge of inequality will be perennial. It is certainly possible to reduce levels of inequality both at an international level (between countries) and nationally (between citizens of the same country), as has been proven at various points in the past 100 years. But any sensible analysis of human history or present-day political conditions will conclude that, while it has peaks and troughs, inequality is a constant aspect of human societies. Efforts to respond to it will therefore be constant as well.

Inequality within, as well as between, countries

But dealing with inter-national inequality is not enough. With our world ever more connected, the conditions must be set not only for gradual global convergence but also for intra-national equality and social cohesion at the country level. Leading politicians and economists are taking inequality seriously in a way that was unthinkable only a few short years ago, when raising the issue marked you out in some circles as a crazy socialist. Alarm bells have been sounding for decades but the financial crisis of the late 2000s poured fuel on that fire, and the coronavirus outbreak pushed inequalities even more into the open. The landmark World Inequality Report (2018) showed how income inequality has increased sharply in nearly all world regions since 1980.[34] The World Economic Forum's Global Risks Report blamed "extreme" wealth inequality for increasing polarisation in societies worldwide, and ranked it among the key underlying trends likely to shape the world over the next decade.[35] The top 10% of income earners accounted for as much as

61% of total national income in the Middle East, the world's most unequal region, but that statistic is out of control pretty much everywhere
else too: 55% in sub-Saharan Africa, Brazil and India; 47% in the US,
Canada and Russia; and even now 41% in China.

The drivers of national inequality are similar across the world,
namely the channelling and coalescing of wealth in the hands of the
few by way of modern capitalist wealth creation, and the inadequacy
of policy to ensure fairer distribution. If current pro-rich models
of economic growth continue, the situation will become even more
socially unbearable. Oxfam reports that in Sao Paulo, Brazil, a person
from the richest neighbourhood will live an average of 25 years more
than someone from one of the poorest areas. In Nepal, a child from a
poor family is three times less likely to reach their fifth birthday than
a child from a rich family.[36]

One of the most important lessons of the MDG era was that while
some progress has been made at a global level, in most countries it has
been uneven and unequal. Income disparities have often worsened,
and particular groups have been left behind, be it for reasons of gender, race, geography or socio-economic class.[37] Worryingly, even what
appear to be important steps forward for equality – as we saw in Latin
America in the first decade of this century – are only pigeon steps given
the scale of the problem, and always seem in danger of reversal. This
time round it was agreed that in the SDG era progress needed to be
even, with the worst-off targeted first – a promise encapsulated in the
now-pervasive phrase, "Leave no-one behind". Not only does income
inequality have its own Goal (SDG10) – confounding sceptics, including the present author, who doubted whether some countries like the
US and UK would sign up to such a thing – but inequality thinking
imbues the SDGs, with a push for disaggregated data to ensure that all
social and income groups benefit from progress.

There is a profound revision of the treatment of gender equality in the
SDGs. The MDG targets were already bold, from equality in the education system to improvement in maternal health, from universal access
to reproductive health services to the elimination of gender inequalities
at work and in political representation. But the gender SDG (5) takes the
challenge to spheres that were previously neglected, insisting on an end
to all forms of discrimination and violence against women and girls and
"all forms of violence" against women. In addition, and perhaps even
more ambitiously, it proposes to "recognize and value unpaid care and
domestic work through the provision of public services, infrastructure
and social protection policies". A more equal society requires institutions that are ever more effective, accountable and transparent and the

SDGs also reflect that, calling for equal access to justice for all, public access to information, protecting fundamental freedoms and providing legal identity, including birth registration.

The challenge for international cooperation in the 21st century is to respond in theory and practice to changing expectations and to expand its narrow poverty focus to incorporate inequality as well. The World Bank has recently expanded its poverty focus to take on board concerns about inequality, emphasising the need to "ensure equal opportunity and reduce inequalities of outcome", and "adopt policies, especially fiscal, wage and social protection policies, to progressively achieve greater equality". Its objective is to ensure that the bottom 40% of the population grow their incomes faster than the national average.

In the same way as the world woke up to racism and sexism in the 20th century and focused its considerable brainpower and solidarity on beginning to do something about it, so in the 21st century it seems plausible that similar movements will be built around other forms of inequality.

Responding to emergencies

So much for human progress, what about sudden emergencies? Throughout history, states have responded with financial, technical and material assistance to crises in other countries. International humanitarian interventions have helped to save millions of lives and provide a basic level of human dignity to people faced with extraordinarily difficult situations. Today, many different types of humanitarian operation are in place around the world, from disaster response when floods, fires, droughts, storms, earthquakes or other catastrophes strike, to support for people affected by war, conflict or other protracted crises. These are usually situations which require a coordinated international response to be effective. "Emergency" aid tends to have a different trajectory to "development" aid – it is about mobilising quickly to respond to sudden, time-limited, crises, rather than addressing chronic problems of poverty, inequality and unsustainable growth. But one thing they have in common is that both strands of cooperation will need increased finance in the years to come. In crisis response, international public finance is often the "first responder", with governments and publicly funded multilateral institutions often banding together to provide funds and launch appeals for more resources.

An estimated 206 million people across 81 countries were deemed to be in need of humanitarian assistance in 2018 and financing for humanitarian operations has more than doubled over the last decade, reaching almost US$29 billion in that year, its highest ever level.[38] Because of international efforts, far fewer people die in environmental disasters than ever before (an estimated 10,300 deaths worldwide in 2018).[39] But, worryingly, experts anticipate that shocks and crises will increase in number and magnitude in the coming decades – we have already seen how climate change is likely to affect the number and severity of extreme weather events, while conflict over resources may increase due to rising inequality. Migration is likely to continue to increase across the globe. Add to this mix crises that are impossible – or very difficult – to predict and the future is unsure to say the least.

There will always be unforeseen emergencies and crises which will require international public finance. And given ever-greater interconnectedness between countries, it will be increasingly in our collective interest to ensure that this emergency response is well-resourced and coordinated. But the money isn't there. The United Nations Office for the Coordination of Humanitarian Affairs (UNOCHA) reported in 2015 that the international community met just 45% of the UN's appeals for humanitarian aid for that year (about US$9 billion of the US$20 billion requested to support 31 separate humanitarian appeals). Despite being the year's most high-profile international emergency, Syria's humanitarian response plan received just 36% of the financial contributions it requested from the international community in 2015. Other appeals fared even worse; the top five underfunded humanitarian appeals in 2015 were: South Sudan (with just 18% of funding requirements met), Senegal (16%), the Sahel (15%), Djibouti (15%) and Gambia (5%). No appeal attracted more than 59% of the amount requested.[40]

Public sector humanitarian aid flows are complemented by private aid flows (e.g. individual donations from members of the public to charities, as well as philanthropic foundations and private company donations): 1 in 4 humanitarian aid dollars now comes from the private sector.[41] But private cannot replace public. Research shows that private aid is more volatile; high-profile emergencies receive widespread media attention, helping to bring much-needed international assistance, including private money, but cash tends to trickle in more slowly for slower onset crises and there are many less widely covered crises, such as conflict and hunger in Africa's Sahel region. Accountability of private actors is also an issue; data on which private actors are spending money where, and for what purposes, is sketchy at best. The capacity of public money to respond to crises is unrivalled. Whether it is refugees fleeing war, floods, droughts, hurricanes, tsunamis, earthquakes, industrial accidents or any other major emergency, international public money is uniquely placed to respond swiftly with the scale of finance needed and a high degree of expertise. Both multilateral organisations and bilateral agencies have developed significant capabilities over the years to respond to complex humanitarian situations. These bodies, in turn, often channel significant resources into non-governmental organisations with long-standing experience in emergency response.

Financial crises – national and international – are particular kinds of emergency that have been pervasive throughout history. However, the frequency and severity of financial crises have increased in recent decades as a consequence of financial deregulation.[42] While the causes are varied (and frequently disputed), the consequences are less contentious: severe declines in output and employment, adverse consequences on government finances, increased costs of essential imports such as food and oil products, decreased remittances and turmoil in financial markets. From a human development perspective, financial crises can reverse important development progress. Numerous studies have explored the social impact of financial crises on the incidence of poverty, levels of crime and domestic violence and education and health indicators.[43]

The 2007–8 financial crisis underscored the distinct role that international public finance plays in crisis response. In 2009, the G20 approved a US$1.1 trillion programme of public financial support to prevent widespread economic collapse – only part of which was concessional. Resources to the International Monetary Fund (IMF) were trebled to US$750 billion. The size of the public sector response was unprecedented in scale and was accompanied by additional public finance mobilised at the national level. This role could not have been fulfilled by private finance – in fact, it was poorly regulated private finance which was one of the root causes of that crisis. As if to prove the point, the global financial crisis led to a significant expansion of shock facilities, including in the IMF, World Bank and the EU. Covid-19-related recessions across the globe are likely to necessitate similar levels of global financial support.

Every financial crisis (national, regional or global) is a reminder that responding to shocks is among the most important roles for **Global Public Investment**. The need to ensure macroeconomic stability at an international level so that individual countries can thrive is well-established, and the role of emergency funding in times of crisis (counter-cyclical) is crucial. The IMF is the largest institution performing this function, although there are also regional entities which provide temporary balance of payments support with varying degrees of success.[44] Love it or hate it, the IMF's job is to be at hand to bail countries out when their economies hit the wall. More recently, the BRICS nations announced the creation of a massive contingency reserve fund. The need for well-resourced contingency financing facilities will always be present.

Higher ambitions, higher costs

Whole books have been written on each of the issues we have looked at in this chapter. First there are the major cross-border issues, such as climate change, sustaining our planet and its ecosystems, migration and global security. Add to that a complete rethink about how ambitious we are for all the countries on the planet, not just ending the worst forms of poverty, but enabling everyone to achieve and thrive in a way now considered normal in the world's wealthier countries – continuing the fight against poverty, reversing growing inequality within countries, ensuring gradual convergence across the world to modern living standards – and you have an even bigger bill on your hands. In a world of Facebook and Twitter, where life in wealthy countries is constantly broadcast to less fortunate parts of the globe, this aspiration is natural. It is impossible to do justice to all these issues here, but I hope the scope of the challenges we face is clear. They are as daunting as they are unprecedented. Global threats and opportunities that require global solutions.

And money. Lots of it. The need to scale-up social and environmental responses will require the mobilisation of unprecedented levels of finance over the long term and will depend on collective international action and collaborations on a scale never seen before. Take those "basic needs", our very first pigeon step towards a more equal world. An analysis carried out in 2019 suggested that an additional US$400 billion per year will be required to finance the basic needs of the 59 poorest countries in the world in health, education, infrastructure, agriculture, ecosystem services, social protection and access to justice.[45] This would not bring countries anywhere close to the kind of living standards expected by people living in the Global North – we are talking the basics. And only in the poorest countries. So add the needs of the other 100 or so countries in the Global South and the bill will rise a great deal more. The World Bank estimates that an additional US$2–3 trillion per year is required to achieve the SDGs, an almost unfathomably large sum of money.[46]

Although many countries are seeking to increase domestic taxation, most cannot be expected to shoulder this burden alone. So where will the additional money come from? Private investment? Philanthropic foundations? Remittances? Yes, all of the above. But what about "aid"? Although the SDG agenda is clearly set out in front of them, with all the fairly obvious implications for scaled-up funding, the aid sector still hasn't got with the programme. Although most countries still publicly call for the 0.7% ODA target to be met, and while lip service is paid to the idea that it remains important, a recurrent undercurrent pervades most of today's development finance discussions – the belief that we have now entered something like the end of the road for aid. Rather than looking to expand it over time, traditional "donors" are looking at ways to draw it down and, eventually, eliminate it altogether. Why? In part, of course, because they are short-sighted and quite keen to keep their money to themselves. But also because they are stuck in an old-fashioned understanding of the function of concessional international public finance. They don't understand how this money can be used to support change across the world, not just in the very poorest countries. That is what we look at in the next chapter.

Notes

1. There are 17 SDGs in total: No Poverty; Zero Hunger; Good Health and Well-being; Quality Education; Gender Equality; Clean Water and Sanitation; Affordable and Clean Energy; Decent Work and Economic Growth; Industry, Innovation and Infrastructure; Reducing Inequality; Sustainable Cities and Communities; Responsible Consumption and Production; Climate Action; Life Below Water; Life On Land; Peace, Justice and Strong Institutions; Partnerships for the Goals.
2. https://www.theguardian.com/global-development/2012/nov/16/mark-malloch-brown-mdgs-nuclear.
3. https://www.ipcc.ch/sr15/.
4. https://www.reuters.com/article/us-climate-change-un/global-temperatures-on-track-for-3-5-degree-rise-by-2100-u-n-idUSKCN1NY186.
5. https://www.undp.org/content/undp/en/home/blog/2017/building-back-better-requires-supportive-international-financing.html.
6. https://www.theguardian.com/global-development/2019/may/16/one-day-disappear-tuvalu-sinking-islands-rising-seas-climate-change.
7. http://news.bbc.co.uk/2/hi/8311838.stm.
8. https://www.theguardian.com/environment/series/the-age-of-extinction.
9. http://www.fao.org/state-of-fisheries-aquaculture/en/.
10. https://www.sciencedirect.com/science/article/abs/pii/S0006320718313636.
11. https://iucnrle.org/.
12. https://www.theguardian.com/environment/2020/mar/10/ecosystems-size-of-amazon-rainforest-can-collapse-within-decades.
13. http://www.lse.ac.uk/GranthamInstitute/publication/the-economics-of-climate-change-the-stern-review/.
14. https://www.vox.com/2018/10/8/17948832/climate-change-global-warming-un-ipcc-report.

15. Guterres Antonio, Think the aid system can cope? It can't, 2015: https://agenda.weforum.org/2015/01/think-the-aid-system-can-cope-it-cant/.
16. The term "international public good" is sometimes preferred to "global public good" because some public goods are regional and therefore not global, but here we use the phrase global public goods because it is better known.
17. There is no internationally agreed definition of the term "global public good" or "international public good". UNDP and the World Bank, for example, each employ slightly different definitions.
18. http://documents.worldbank.org/curated/en/297241468339565863/pdf/PUB20800REPLACEMENT0WDR01978.pdf.
19. All data from World Development Indicators online, World Bank.
20. World Bank 2018, Piecing together the poverty puzzle.
21. https://www.wider.unu.edu/publication/estimates-impact-covid-19-global-poverty.
22. The World Bank has a more specific aim to reduce extreme poverty to 3% of the global population by 2030.
23. Fukuda Parr, in Alonso et al. (2014).
24. 1978 World Development Report, World Bank.
25. Personal communication.
26. Sumner (2013), "Aid Agencies of the Future." The Economist, 3 June, http://www.economist.com/blogs/feastandfamine/2013/06/aid-agencies-future.
27. https://www.indexmundi.com/facts/indicators/SH.STA.STNT.ZS/rankings.
28. Thresholds nearer $5 or $10/day would better imply resilience against the possibility of falling back into extreme destitution. See Sumner (2013).
29. Personal communication at a meeting of the UN Development Cooperation Forum.
30. https://www.kateraworth.com/doughnut/.
31. See www.fao.org/state-of-food-security-nutrition/en/. Other research suggests this is an undercount. See Pogge (2015).
32. For more detail on the SDGs see UNDP (2016) Transitioning from the MDGs to the SDGs
33. https://www.understandingglasgow.com/indicators/health/trends/male_life_expectancy_trends_in_scottish_cities.
34. World Inequality Report, 2018: https://wir2018.wid.world/.
35. World Economic Forum, Global Risks 2017.
36. Oxfam 2019, Public Good or Private Wealth, https://www.oxfam.org/en/research/public-good-or-private-wealth.
37. See, for instance, https://www.savethechildren.org.uk/content/dam/global/reports/education-and-child-protection/every-last-child.pdf.
38. http://devinit.org/wp-content/uploads/2019/09/GHA-report-2019.pdf.
39. See: http://worldpopulationreview.com/countries/life-expectancy-by-country/ and Statista, The Statistics Portal, Number of deaths from natural disaster events globally from 2000 to 2018: https://www.statista.com/statistics/510952/number-of-deaths-from-natural-disasters-globally/.
40. All data from Financial tracking service, Humanitarian aid contributions reported this year https://fts.unocha.org/.

41. High-Level Panel on Humanitarian Financing Report to the Secretary-General (2016) Too important to fail—addressing the humanitarian financing gap, p15

42. Indeed, much literature has shown that the frequency and severity of financial crises has increased since the 1970s when the Bretton Woods fixed exchange rate system collapsed. Bordo et al. (2000) Financial Crises: Lessons from the last 120 years

43. For instance http://www.unicef.org/socialpolicy/files/social_consequences_of_the_financial_crisis_in_asia.pdf and http://gsp.sagepub.com/content/9/1_suppl/79.full.pdfandhttp://www.undp.org/content/undp/en/home/ourwork/povertyreduction/projects_and_initiatives/projects_psia_economic_crisis/.

44. They include the FLAR (Fondo Latinoamericano de Reservas) in Latin America, the Arab Monetary Fund and the Chiang Mai Initiative in Asia.

45. https://www.unsdsn.org/new-report-estimates-sdg-financing-needs-for-59-of-the-worlds-lowest-income-countries.

46. http://documents.worldbank.org/curated/en/492461543350814564/pdf/132533-WP-BackgroundPaperforGInvestorForumweb.pdf.

4 FUNCTION

From last resort to first priority

- *Traditional analysis*: **Foreign aid** is only necessary in exceptional circumstances to fill a financial gap. It should be phased out when other finances are available.

- *New paradigm*: **Global Public Investment** has a unique set of characteristics and cannot simply be replaced by other types of finance.

So the challenges of tomorrow will be just as urgent and complex as those of yesterday, maybe more so if we allow ourselves to be as ambitious as a decent, non-stingy, moral analysis implies. There is no sense in thinking that the work of international development and cooperation is coming to an end. On the contrary, it is just beginning. Responding to these challenges will be expensive – we are going to need to find much more money to pay for the better world we want. But how much of that money needs to be public, rather than private? And how much is needed from international, rather than domestic, sources? Does it need to be concessional, rather than earning a financial return? In short, how important is **Global Public Investment** in responding to the global challenges we have discussed? What is its FUNCTION in the 21st century?

Public money is special money

In April 2015, a few months before the SDG agenda was acclaimed in New York, UN member states met in a conference centre in Addis Ababa to discuss how the hell to finance it.[1] Never had such an ambitious agenda been put to the world's nations before, and something out of the ordinary was required. The World Bank (along with the IMF and the regional development banks) contributed a short discussion paper whose catchy title soon become part of the development lexicon:

Table 4.1 Eight potential sources of finance for development (with examples)

	Public	Private (for profit)	Philanthropic	Household
Domestic	National taxes Natural resource revenues	Bank credit Public-private partnerships	National charities Corporate philanthropy	Household spending
International	ODA & SSC Non-concessional loans	Foreign direct investment Foreign market loans	International NGOs Philanthropic foundations	Remittances

"From Billions to Trillions: Transforming Development Finance".[2] Most people agreed (and still do) that to achieve the SDGs the international community needs to find not just billions but trillions of dollars. If the MDG era was characterised by an overreliance on the idea of "aid" to help deliver global development objectives, this time around no such limited vision would be allowed. ODA quantities fall far short of the "trillions" required to achieve the SDGs, so the focus on ODA which dominated the MDG era needed to be balanced with a search for other funds?

For the purposes of simplicity, there are, broadly, eight categories of development finance, each with various sub-categories. Sources of finance can be divided into national and international,[3] and then further divided into public, private, philanthropic and household. Table 4.1 gives a couple of examples of each type of finance. Of course, there are myriad variants and overlaps within these eight categories (including the "blended" finance used in Public-Private Partnerships (PPPs) and co-financed aid projects) but this is a useful framing of the subject for now.

It is (obviously) neither possible nor desirable for international public finance (IPF) (the bottom left-hand corner of the table) to cover even the MDG objectives, let alone the SDGs, so it is self-evident that all sources of funds need to be maximised if the world is going to get anywhere near meeting the SDG targets – domestic taxes, private finance, philanthropic funds, remittances, everything. And indeed, busy efforts are underway to maximise these other sources. But while the international community is pulling out all the stops to increase other types of development finance to support the delivery of the immensely ambitious SDGs, to gather trillions not just billions of dollars, it is at best ambiguous on the future of ODA. Why? Why would an important piece of the funding jigsaw be deprioritised just when ambitions are being stepped up?

Most of the talk is of private finance. *Public* resources for international concerns are scarce, it is argued, and *private* finance – which is much larger in volume terms – must play a much more prominent role. It is true that, in volume terms, IPF cannot compete with the much larger quantities of private finance. Foreign direct investment (FDI) to the Global South has averaged well over US$600 billion since 2010. Most countries are also able to access international capital markets in a way that was previously impossible; total external long-term debt stocks in the Global South reached over US$5.5 trillion in 2018, up from US$1.7 trillion in 2000. Migrant remittances to the Global South are also significant and were estimated to be almost US$500 billion in 2018, coming from hundreds of millions of migrant workers across the world. The potential of institutional investors and sovereign wealth funds to provide finance which could be invested in long-term development initiatives is also growing. Global capital markets represent an astonishing US$200 trillion in financial assets[4]; in 2019, the Norwegian Government Pension Fund alone held over US$1 trillion. Reorienting even a small proportion of these resources towards sustainable development objectives could have an enormous impact.

In contrast, ODA from the 30 OECD member countries amounted to a little over US$150 billion in 2019, and South-South Cooperation is considerably less, although it continues to expand. The superior scale of international private finance compared to its public counterpart means that high expectations are being placed on the private sector to play an increasingly major role in the financing of sustainable development in the post-2015 era. But a strange fallacy seems to have taken hold, a kind of sleight of hand, a contradiction, an ambiguity. Just because other sources of development finance are increasingly important, it does not follow that concessional IPF ceases to be important at all which, despite lip service being paid to the ongoing importance of ODA, is the basis of most of today's development finance debates. In fact, according to a different logic, the scarcity of concessional IPF makes it even more valuable.

From filling gaps to overcoming traps

"What is relevant is not only the direct effect of the *amount* of resources... but the role that international cooperation may play in modifying the framework of *incentives* in which agents operate". Jose Antonio Alonso, Universidad Complutense

Development finance analysts like to measure something they call the "financing gap". The financing gap is the difference, according to their calculations, between the amount of money needed to deliver a particular good (such as good quality education, or comprehensive measles immunisation) and the amount of money currently available. When the amount of money required has been calculated, they set about looking for it. If one type (say, domestic resources from taxation) is unavailable, another is sought (say, private finance from international banks). Or maybe increasing remittances can be mobilised? Or other sources of development finance. If there is not enough domestic or private finance, then, and only then, foreign aid must step in as a "last resort". Conversely, as other forms of finance become more available they can fill the gap left behind by reducing aid, so that over time only a rump of emergency international public cash is left for crises. Given the scale of the challenge the world faces today, and given that concessional IPF is small in quantity relative to domestic and private money, which many countries in the Global South are today able to access in new ways, it is perhaps understandable that many in the development sector are focusing on the bigger pots.

But this kind of thinking is seriously flawed. All dollars are not equal, and private money cannot simply replace public money as some appear to hope. Money is not interchangeable in this way. It is not just the quantity of money that matters; the type of money matters too. The characteristics of different sources of finance are critical to their role in financing development. Foreign investment could hardly be more different from revenue raised from income taxes, which in turn is very different from international aid, and philanthropy, and so on. Each has a distinct role in the effort to raise living standards equitably and sustainably. **Global Public Investment** has unique characteristics that make it very important in the mix of funds available for development even if, compared to other sources of development finance, there is relatively less of it.

The differences between public and private money are well understood by the general public when it comes to the national level. No-one would ever argue at the national level that public money is interchangeable with private money, that it doesn't matter whether health or education, parks or prisons or infrastructure, are financed publicly or privately, just as long as they are financed. We all know that different types of money lead to different outcomes. Private finance does a poor job at financing public goods, for instance, and it does not *a priori* focus on delivering government priorities or link strongly to human rights. And if public money for, say, health or education, were particularly scarce (as it is in many countries), no one would argue that limited amount of public resource is therefore irrelevant and can be allowed slowly to dry up; on the contrary, it would be guarded as a crucial resource and plans would be drawn up to increase it over time. So it is at the international level; precisely because **Global Public Investment** is scarce, all the more should it be nurtured and defended. But this fundamental distinction between "private" and "public" funding is routinely overlooked in SDG financing discussions, which focus on the "financing gap".

Filling gaps in the budgets of poorer countries is, of course, part of the reason **Global Public Investment** is so important. Where national revenue is not enough to cover necessary expenditure, **Global Public Investment** can help increase the supply of public goods and services in a given country. And that gap, as we argued in the last chapter, is actually much bigger than is sometimes acknowledged. Many national budgets are still insufficient to provide basic services, let alone all the additional spending required to fulfil SDG-level ambitions. In its 2019 report calling for a new Global Green New Deal, the UN calculates that for a sample of 31 countries in the Global South, "meeting basic SDG-related investment requirements to address poverty, nutrition, health and education goals, would result in an increase of public debt-to-GDP ratios from around 47 per cent at present to no less than 185 per cent, on average, if current expenditure and financing patterns prevail. Alternatively, to achieve these SDGs without an increase in existing debt-to-GDP ratios by 2030, developing countries would have to grow at an average annual rate of almost 12 per cent per year. Clearly, neither scenario is remotely realistic". The report estimates that improved domestic resource mobilisation could raise "between one fifth and one half of this SDG financing gap", that international private finance is "not anywhere near on track to provide the trillions needed to close the remaining gap" and so concludes that substantially scaling up public international development finance, including through development assistance and debt relief, should therefore be an a urgent priority".[5]

This is where a rethink is required by the international community. Clearly the ideal is that countries finance the bulk of their expenditure, particularly given the volatility of external flows, but if we are serious about raising the funds needed to go beyond a poverty focus and respond to inequality and unsustainability, we are going to have to accept that they are simply not available in-country or from private sources. The sums required are simply too vast. And the lazy call for private money to come riding to the rescue has not been heeded.[6]

Global Public Investment for the purposes of filling gaps is certain to be needed for many decades to come, given the scale of the challenge. In the era of an (almost) exclusive poverty focus, it was argued that "donors" needed to commit 0.7% of GNI to ODA. How much more will be needed to meet the SDG targets!

So, yes, **Global Public Investment** is still definitely about gap filling. But it is not *just* about that. As well as being the finance of last resort, it should also often be the finance of first resort (to use Mazzucato's phrase), the first thought, the best option even when other types of money are also available. Why? Because of its unique characteristics. Size isn't everything. Different sources of finance can be effective in meeting different needs and cannot simply be replaced by another source of money. Just because the quantities of IPF are relatively small, does not mean that its contribution is unimportant. Whether the level of cooperation is large or small, the incentivising effect is a crucial part of **Global Public Investment**, emphasising certain actions in recipient countries or organisations that otherwise may not have been prioritised. This may be support to official sectors (e.g. PPPs in infrastructure and support to revenue collection agencies) or non-official, such as the focus on women's rights and the need for a strong civil society. It can be done through capacity building, training, temporary core support, provision of information, exchange of experiences, technical assistance and so on. For example, a focus on social policies might lead to an emphasis on the quality of economic growth rather than GDP growth as a simple target. It could focus attention more on investment in human and institutional capacity building, governance and the rule of law from which a stronger foundation for growth can be built. Criteria for determining "good policies" might be shared with relevant parts of the international community and implemented in transparent ways.

An evaluation characterised ODA spent in Colombia in the first years of this century as follows: *"The evaluation found that in certain fields – such as the environment, institutional strengthening, and productive system support, as well as problems related to the struggle against inequality, internal displacement and human rights violations – the selective use of aid financing, expertise and shared experience was a 'determining factor in achieving better development results'".*[7] Not just a factor, a *determining* factor. How can that be if IPF is effectively irrelevant at low levels, the mantra we so often hear in development finance debates. Colombia receives just 0.3% of its GNI in ODA, a tiny amount and a figure that hasn't fluctuated much since the 1970s (but is now under serious pressure as "donors" begin to walk away from a country still riven by conflict and inequality, with a poor health system and weak educational outcomes). But the nature of ODA, its unique characteristics as a source of finance, has made this small resource a hugely important one. This is the function we could call overcoming traps – whereby it is not so much the quantity of money that matters, but the way it is used.[8] It is recognised that many so-called middle-income countries are caught in developmental traps that restrict their ability to progress – which is one of the reasons **Global Public Investment** is for all countries, middle-income as well as low-income (insofar as these terms are still useful.)[9]

From quantity to unique characteristics

It is not either-or; global public money is needed both to fill gaps and to help overcome traps. Taking these two crucial functions together, there are (at least) five critical characteristics that mark **Global Public Investment** out as a necessary complement to other types of finance in achieving sustainable development: Motivation, Accountability, Flexibility, Concessionality and Expertise. Other types of money may share these specific attributes some of the time; it is the particular balance of these characteristics in given situations that makes **Global Public Investment** unique.

Motivation

The first critical and unique attribute of **Global Public Investment** is its motivation. While private spending is primarily interested in benefiting the spender (be that a household or an investment firm), public spending is supposed to benefit society as a whole. In other words, its primary purpose is the public good, not profit. Whereas private banks and financing institutions expect to make a decent financial return on the money they risk, contributors of **Global Public Investment** do not – although they expect to see social returns aplenty.

In reality, of course, altruistic motives are almost always in tension with self-interest. Altruism, or international solidarity, is about the moral obligation of wealthier countries and peoples to assist fellow human beings in poorer countries. Self-interest is about the political, security, economic and commercial considerations of the provider nation; for example, financial assistance may be used to "buy" political allegiance, to secure access to resources or to expand the provider country's exports. In fact, it might be useful to think of the motivations behind **Global Public Investment** as a spectrum, with altruism at one end and the self-interest of the provider at the other. The motives of any particular contribution lie somewhere along this spectrum. Slap in the middle of the spectrum is a perfect blend of mutual benefit whereby both the provider and receiver of international cooperation benefit in good measure. Acting out of enlightened self-interest means intervening in issues that impact the contributor as well as the recipient, albeit usually less directly, issues such as global health threats, climate change, and transnational crime and terrorism which have negative spillovers across borders.[10]

Interventions can have multiple objectives, delivering several outcomes simultaneously. For example, funds intended to improve the environment (such as carbon sequestration achieved through the preservation of forests) can have important socio-economic spillover benefits (for example through the development of ecotourism or other business opportunities). Or a country may supply funds to another primarily to cement a political alliance, but the funds may have parallel developmental objectives.

Importantly, while the motivations of public finance at the international level are similar to domestic public finance, in that they are not motivated by private profit, there are also important differences, because international considerations come into play, particularly the desire to support internationally agreed public objectives. Thus, while public spending at the national level can flip to support different agendas when a new government comes to power, at the international level the objectives set at the UN and other global membership bodies tend to be longer term and binding for governments of all stripes. This collective will, expressed in international treaties and declarations, is important as it often expresses the best of humanity, its highest ideals and ambitions. We define **Global Public Investment** as motivated by public motives taking the term "public" not just to refer to the *source* of the funds, but also to the *objective* for which they are used. If it isn't, it doesn't count. Clearly that is hard to actually police. But it is what we are working towards.

Accountability

Related to the motivations of IPF is its second major defining criteria: accountability. Every different source of development finance has its own accountability tree. Private funds ultimately need to turn a profit, and reports will be sent to business owners and shareholders. Philanthropic funds need to satisfy those providing the money, be they dotcom billionaires and their close family, or the general public who just give a few coins passing by a collecting tin. Domestic resources need to be held accountable by domestic tax payers. **Global Public Investment** is different again. Its accountability trail can pass through implementing organisations through to elected politicians and finally to taxpayers again, but this time of other countries. None of these accountability systems is perfect, but they are all different. Each has its particularities that make it strong in some aspects and weaker in others. Sometimes it is great that only one or two people can decide how to spend the money of a philanthropic organisation – it makes getting quick money behind an important issue much easier. But sometimes big money needs to be managed more democratically.

Global Public Investment can provide flexible funds for innovative or risky activities that otherwise might not take place, in part because recipient countries might not be able to use their own funds, for which they have to answer to their own people, but can use global funds, whose accountability trail is different. Obviously, international interventions generally need to support national democratic strategies and directions, but that doesn't mean international pressure can't also sometimes be a good thing. The key is that decisions need to be as fairly and expertly made as possible, with the interests of those who really need support at heart. That means that governance structures need to change with the times, to help manage complex mixed motivations and hold powerful decision makers accountable – an issue we come to in Chapter 6.

Flexibility

The third attribute of **Global Public Investment** is its flexibility. While the development sector talks as if raising levels of IPF is a near-impossibility while increases in "private flows" and "domestic resource mobilisation" are a foregone conclusion, the reality is that the latter are often equally hard to come by. Countries differ widely in their capacities to attract and access various forms of external finance. For instance, FDI is heavily concentrated in middle-income countries and resource rich low-income countries, while fragile and conflict-affected countries tend to struggle to raise external funds, as do some small islands and low-income countries with a low natural resource endowment, lacking the wealth and income streams to repay investors. Even in countries with stronger economies, private finance remains concentrated in specific sectors (such as natural resource extraction and exploitation of comparative advantage in labour-intensive industries) where expected risk-adjusted returns are higher. Several areas crucial for sustainable development therefore fail to attract sufficient private financing, such as social services, long-term investments (in particular in infrastructure), high-risk investments (such as research, science and new technologies and financing for small and medium-sized enterprises) and financing for global public goods (such as dealing with communicable diseases like coronavirus). This comes as no real surprise since most private capital is driven by the profit motive.

Private capital is often simply unaffordable or provided at maturities which would make longer-term investments in areas such as infrastructure untenable. International capital flows are highly mobile and have become more short term in orientation; in the United States, for example, the average holding period for stocks fell from 8 years in the 1960s to 6 months in 2010.[11] The consequence is that it tends to leave many countries and sectors severely underserved. Worse, when some countries have tried to bring in private funds, they have simply accentuated vulnerability to economic and financial crises.

Global Public Investment can be more flexible than other types of finance, depending on context. Where private capital flows are pro-cyclical, IPF performs an important counter-cyclical function and can be mobilised both at scale and at speed (where sufficient political will exists). In periods of economic shock, commercial loans can dry-up and anti-cyclical funds may be required rapidly. The 2008 financial crisis is a case in point. Faced with what Ben Bernanke, former Head of the United States Federal Reserve described as, "the worst financial crisis in global history, including the Great Depression"[12] – this was before Covid-19 – G20 leaders convened in London and overnight trebled the resources available to the IMF to enable it to help countries deal with the fall-out from the crisis.

Concessionality

Global Public Investment's fourth crucial aspect is its concessionality. Concessional, when referring to finance, basically means "cheaper than the market." The OECD has a complicated (and recently changed) definition of "concessional", but most non-OECD countries don't use it and tend to be quite opaque about the terms of their financial transfers. The result is confusion. However one defines it, only a portion of IPF flows can be considered concessional. When we say IPF we are talking here about financial interventions by a nation-state or multilateral organisation acting on behalf of nation-states to secure desired public policy outcomes outside the boundaries of that state.

Broadly speaking, it can consist of grants (i.e. transfers made in cash, goods or services for which no repayment is required), loans (at a large variety of terms, some concessional, some not), equity investments (directed largely at productive sectors) and guarantees (e.g. export credit guarantees). While non-concessional IPF is often intended to further public objectives, it is by definition also intended to bring a return to the contributor. In fact, even supposedly concessional funds have regularly in the past led to poor countries becoming indebted to lenders as they struggle to pay back "cheap loans" on time, generating fines and accumulated interest. That's why, when it comes to **Global Public Investment**, concessional should mean free: non-reimbursable, not seeking a financial or political return of any kind, but simply an investment in progress for the peoples of the world. That makes it a very special kind of money.

Expertise

The fifth attribute of **Global Public Investment** to bring out here (there may be others) is expertise. It tends to be managed by entities with specific knowledge in supporting development, including access to technical expertise and knowledge networks. While recipients are keen to move on from situations in which this expertise has been used aggressively to impose heavy and wrong-headed conditions in return for receiving loans (especially when managed by the major US-based international financial institutions) they appreciate the added value of expertise on development issues. For example, China as an upper middle-income economy and one of the world's fastest growing countries over recent years arguably no longer "needs" to borrow resources from multilateral development banks such as the World Bank and the Asian Development Bank (ADB). Yet it chooses to do so for a variety of reasons. With loans totalling US$31.5 billion, China is the ADB's second-largest borrower.[13] Many of the projects combine support for infrastructure with areas such as technical and vocational education and training as well as environmental improvement, areas in which the multilateral development banks have built up considerable expertise. This suggests that it is not simply the cash that matters. Being an important provider and recipient of financing from these institutions can also provide countries with valuable political leverage within them. In humanitarian crises, as well, multilateral organisations and bilateral agencies have developed significant capabilities and expertise to respond to what are often complex and protracted crisis situations.

What does that mean in practice?

These five characteristics make **Global Public Investment** desirable to governments and civil society alike. Far from being a last resort, it has particular characteristics which mean that it is sometimes the single most important source of finance available to meet a specific need, in all country types, not just the poorest countries. We have already looked at some of the sectors where it will be crucial in the years ahead (such as health, education, emergencies, conservation) but there are many others, including actions to reduce asymmetries in business practices (e.g. reforms of the global financial system or international trade), investments to incentivise international agreements on money laundering, illicit trade and arms trading (so as to reflect the true global costs of such activities for global peace and security), and compensating for market failures to supply long-term finance for sustainable projects.

The fact that the two most comprehensive accounts of the role of IPF to date were written in 1992 and 2006 respectively demonstrates how much more work is required to develop this concept. In 1992, Ruben Mendez showed in *"International Public Finance: New Perspectives on Global Relations"* that there is much more to IPF than "aid". He contended that the world's challenges are so immense and interconnected that they require concerted action and concerted public resources. The flow of public resources for international challenges is however voluntary, politically motivated and patchwork in nature. What is needed is a new institutional framework, resourced through mandatory contributions, which can more effectively mobilise and allocate resources to international problems.[14] In 2006, in *"The New Public Finance"*, Inge Kaul and Pedro Conceição explored how governments individually and collectively channel public and private financing and asked how the process could be made more inclusive and efficient to respond to global policy challenges (such as development, communicable disease control and climate change).[15]

Take global infrastructure, where investment needs are estimated at upwards of a walloping US$6.3 trillion per year over the next decade.[16] With populations growing, some estimate that annual spending on infrastructure in the Global South will need to double to about US$2 trillion each year, with electricity, water and transport accounting for the bulk of this.[17] Current spending on infrastructure is mostly financed by domestic budgets. In the long run, the economic impact of infrastructural development will be positive, via an increase in productivity and energy efficiency, the reduction of transportation and communication costs, strengthening regional integration and a more adequate supply of social services. But in the short term, it will be expensive, especially if it is to be "green" – up to 15% additional upfront costs according to one influential study.[18] And if we fail to "green" the economy, our quest for global fairness could worsen climate change and other environmental problems. Despite their importance for development (i.e. their high socio-economic returns), infrastructure projects are often not considered financially viable, with expected revenues unable to cover project costs. The long-term nature of investments combined with other associated risks (macroeconomic, political, operational) means that securing adequate infrastructure financing from the private sector can be challenging. Many projects cannot be realised without some form of public support. **Global Public Investment** – with its critical five attributes – represents the start-up funds many countries need to finance their development plans. In most countries, the multilateral development banks are the main source of financing for infrastructure investment.

Looking beyond infrastructure towards other measures required to stimulate the economy, during the early stages of their industrialisation countries generally need to protect and subsidise fragile domestic industries until they can open up to competition without domestic output being swamped by imports. A possible role for **Global Public Investment**, given its attributes, is building partnerships focused on technology and knowledge transfer to provide added value to local output and create the necessary conditions for local entrepreneurs to compete favourably with foreign competitors. The informal sector generates the bulk of jobs created in poorer countries; in Africa it accounts for 75% of job creation in agriculture, craft industry, mutual savings, social protection, primary healthcare and other areas. Economic revival will require a large injection of **GPI** in the informal sector to modernise it and insert it in the mainstream of the economy while conserving its creativity and flexibility. It could help finance small- and medium-sized projects such as sugar refineries, paper mills and grain mills, forestry and irrigation, health, education, agriculture and sports projects.

Research, science and technology[19]

One crucial area worth looking at in a bit more detail is the world of research, mobilising knowledge and innovation for global progress, from global health to the much-needed "green revolution".[20] Much more funding for new technologies, research, science and innovation will be essential to drive the transformation we need, and **Global Public Investment** will have a critical role to play, enabling countries to tackle specific shared challenges, promoting economic and industrial competitiveness, and ensuring a large public stake in the creation of new knowledge and technologies. Governments need to be more proactive in the use of public resources to support researchers and scientists, including with more cross-border collaborations. Notwithstanding the important contribution that private sources of finance can make, public resources have historically played a key role in creating and shaping markets, and public sector agencies are especially able to take on risks in the most capital-intensive and high-risk areas. The magnitude of the knowledge divide between countries, and the need to focus on structural economic transformation, makes this an urgent task, but initiatives launched during recent decades fall short of meeting the challenge.

It is not just that there is not enough research into health, climate and other sustainable development issues; it's also that much of that there is is privately owned. The intellectual property regime militates against sharing technological advances – investing more public money in research would help overcome this problem.[21] Although the institutional arrangements associated with intellectual property rights have been designed to allow the private appropriation of knowledge, knowledge is intrinsically a public good. The revival of interest in South-South Cooperation has placed knowledge exchange firmly at the heart of the development agenda.

In the current era, with the digital society in full swing, there are three main sets of activities that require **Global Public Investment** to achieve global development objectives. First, to finance scientific research to generate new technologies and to update conventional technologies. Competitions, global challenge funds, prizes, advance purchases and similar financial instruments could be used to mobilise talent and creativity anywhere in the world to address problems such as the development of vaccines for tropical diseases, conservation of biodiversity, unconventional energy sources, water and sanitation supply and improving agricultural productivity. Second, to finance capacity building initiatives in the Global South to acquire, absorb and adapt scientific development, and to begin generating home-grown technological responses to development problems. There is a wealth of experience accumulated during the last five decades on what works in this field, and there have been several proposals to establish financial facilities for this purpose. Third, these financing initiatives should be complemented with measures to facilitate access to the pool of existing technologies without restrictions to countries in the Global South, meaning changes in international intellectual property regimes, particularly for technologies and innovations that address basic needs and human survival issues.

Scientific research is becoming more globalised and collaborative, and developments in science and technology are increasingly the result of this collaboration. More and more countries are building scientific capabilities and funding world science and, correspondingly, a growing proportion of projects and publications are the result of collaborations between scientists from a mix of nations. National boundaries are of diminishing importance for scientific enquiries. The European Union is leading the way, with over EUR80 billion made available between 2014 and 2020 to support scientific enquiry, discoveries and innovation across European countries and beyond as part of the Horizon 2020 initiative.[22] But while countries can benefit from increased dynamism in world science, it may be more difficult for governments to demonstrate the direct domestic benefit for every dollar spent. That makes the **Global Public Investment** approach more attractive i.e. rather than an additional expenditure to be justified every time to voters, it would simply be a norm that all countries fulfil.

Writing in the Lancet in March 2020, Sarah Dalglish, a global health expert, wrote that, "The global health system is based in large part on technical assistance and capacity building by the US, the UK, and other rich countries, whose response has been delayed and sclerotic at best..." She pointed to a report by Global Health 50/50 showing that 85% of global organisations working in health have headquarters in Europe and North America and over 80% of global health leaders are nationals of high-income countries. "Relatively little has been heard of the African veterans of the Ebola epidemics," she noted, despite their expertise. A new "Global Knowledge Facility" tasked with bridging the knowledge divide between rich and poor nations could herald a new generation of international cooperation on research. Those responsible for the management of such a facility should be free from interference by political or commercial interests and be given autonomy to operate without excessive and cumbersome controls, but with clearly defined lines of accountability to all stakeholders participating in the scheme. The corresponding research and development activities should be carried out jointly through arrangements that involve all countries and regions. CGIAR (formerly the *Consultative Group on International Agricultural Research*) is an example of the kind of organisation the world could see much more of in the years ahead.

Small but crucial

Private actors are increasingly entering and changing the game in development finance, bringing money and new ways of working. International private capital flows have also become more sophisticated and diversified and offer a rich range of financial products and services. The countries of the world now live in a "new age of choice" as far as development financing options are concerned.[23] However, while there are growing pockets of socially and environmentally conscious investors, most private capital has to be cajoled quite hard into serving sustainable development better. **Global Public Investment** can play a crucial role in bringing private funds forward to invest in public-interest projects, and it can help catalyse, leverage, mobilise and direct private finance through matching funds, guarantees, insurance, advance purchase agreements, interest rate subsidies on loans and capital contributions to multilateral development institutions. But private cannot replace public. The role of concessional IPF will remain crucial not just because it is available when other types of finance are not (filling gaps) but because of its inherent characteristics, furthering mutually agreed international goals, flexible and available counter-cyclically and in parts of the world where there is little profit to be made, bringing with it principles of social and environmental integrity and the expertise of public servants (overcoming traps). As with the other paradigm shifts, it is not either-or but both-and.

The gap-filling function of **Global Public Investment** will remain important, far more so than many currently think, given that traditional analyses are quite stingy in what they consider countries to "need". And quantity will still matter – some of the challenges faced by the world will require very significant investments. But as other sources of development finance become gradually more available to all countries except the most malfunctioning, the trend to focus on the quality of the financing will continue in the new era, and the development characteristics of **Global Public Investment**, rather than just its availability, will be all-important. While this will be a new concept in some circles, it has been the reality for many years, especially when recipient countries have relatively higher per capita incomes. It is also one of the main concepts behind the recent rise of South-South Cooperation, which emphasises not the recipient country's absolute lack of funds, but the possibility that it might benefit from shared expertise and technology, with the finance coming in to support that exchange.

There is near-consensus that this is the moment to take international efforts to promote global development to a new level. But while the challenges the world faces are mostly recognised, including in the SDG agenda - our roadmap to a fairer and more sustainable world - the resources required are not being mobilised. We have the shopping list, but no-one seems to have remembered their wallet? In fact, concessional IPF is being deprioritised. Why? Despite its demonstrable value and the obvious need, the assumption persists that it should be steadily reduced as countries pass that famous income threshold. Economists in high places argue that the importance of IPF is falling in the world, as it declines in size relative to other financial flows, but the opposite is actually true. As economies grow the importance of IPF does not diminish, but it does evolve. Of course, **Global Public Investment** will only ever be a small part of the response to inequality and unsustainable development, just as aid has been a bit part player in the fight against extreme poverty. But it is an important part nonetheless, and it can't just be replaced by other types of money.

Notes

1. While it was, unfortunately, more plan than action, the Addis Ababa Action Agenda did help to bring out some of the key features of a new financing settlement in the years ahead. Areas of focus included tax (the need to raise domestic resources in a more effective manner), the role of the private sector and the role of philanthropy.
2. Development Committee (Joint Ministerial Committee of the Boards of Governors of the Bank and the Fund on the Transfer of Real Resources to Developing Countries) (2015), From Billions to Trillions: Transforming Development Finance Post-2015 Financing for Development: Multilateral Development Finance.
3. Sub-categories here include sub-national and regional.
4. http://documents.worldbank.org/curated/en/492461543350814564/pdf/132533-WP-BackgroundPaperforGInvestorForumweb.pdf.
5. https://unctad.org/en/pages/PublicationWebflyer.aspx?publicationid=2526.
6. https://www.odi.org/publications/11303-blended-finance-poorest-countries-need-better-approach.
7. Wood et al. (2011), The Evaluation of the **Paris** Declaration: Final Report: https://www.oecd.org/derec/dacnetwork/48152078.pdf.
8. https://effectivecooperation.org/wp-content/uploads/2014/04/Recipients-and-Contributors-EXECUTIVE-SUMMARY.pdf.
9. https://papers.ssrn.com/sol3/papers.cfm?abstract_id=3526261.
10. Sagasti, Bezanson and Prada (2005) and Gulrajani, N., et al. (2019).
11. https://www.un.org/development/desa/dpad/wp-content/uploads/sites/45/2017wesp_chap3_en.pdf.

12. Forbes, Ben Bernanke: The 2008 Financial Crisis Was Worse Than the Great Depression, 2014: http://www.forbes.com/sites/timworstall/2014/08/27/ben-bernanke-the-2008-financial-crisis-was-worse-than-the-great-depression/.
13. Asian Development Bank & People's Republic of China, Fact Sheet, 2015: http://www.adb.org/sites/default/files/publication/27789/prc.pdf.
14. Mendez, R. (1992), International Public Finance. A New Perspective on Global Relations.
15. Kaul, I and Conceição P (2006), The New Public Finance, Responding to Global Challenges.
16. https://www.oecd.org/env/cc/g20-climate/Technical-note-estimates-of-infrastructure-investment-needs.pdf.
17. For further information, see: Bhattacharya A. et al (2012) *"Infrastructure for development: meeting the challenge"* (2012).
18. "Between 10 and 15% of the required infrastructure investment could be attributed to making such investment sustainable, by ensuring lower-emissions, higher efficiency and resilience to climate change". http://www.lse.ac.uk/GranthamInstitute/wp-content/uploads/2014/03/PP-infrastructure-for-development-meeting-the-challenge.pdf.
19. This work draws heavily on the ideas of Francisco Sagasti and his team.
20. What will it take to get us a Green Revolution? Mazzucato Mariana, Semieniuk Gregor and Watson Jim, 2015: https://www.sussex.ac.uk/webteam/gateway/file.php?name=what-will-it-take-to-get-us-a-green-revolution.pdf&site=264.
21. http://www.guardian.co.uk/global-development/poverty-matters/2011/jul/15/aid-money-research-clean-technology.
22. EU Horizon, 2020: http://ec.europa.eu/programmes/horizon2020/en/what-horizon-2020.
23. This term was coined by ODI. https://www.odi.org/projects/2782-age-choice-developing-countries-new-aid-landscape

5   GEOGRAPHY

From North-South to universal

- *Traditional analysis*: Wealthy countries give **Foreign Aid** to poorer ones.

- *New paradigm*: All countries should contribute to **Global Public Investment**, according to ability, and all can benefit from it, according to need.

So far we have established that the challenges facing the world are great, and that international public money in the shape of **Global Public Investment** should be a critical part of the international response. In this chapter, we are going to ask who should contribute to this effort, and who should benefit, in a context of shifting global power and responsibility.

More money, more power

Our world today is very different from how it was as recently as 20 years ago. As wealth continues to shift, largely to the South and East, power and influence reside in an expanding number of places. Since the turn of the millennium it has not been the world's so-called "developed" countries but "developing" countries that have been driving global economic growth. The most important group of emerging economies in recent years are the so-called BRICS – Brazil, Russia, India, China and South Africa – and most attention has focused on the rapid economic advances of China, which has helped lift millions of people out of extreme income poverty over a short period of time. These power-houses are closely followed by a second tier of acronymed countries including the CIVETS[1] and the Next 11[2]. According to an analysis by HSBC, lesser known candidates for global power such as Peru and the Philippines are among those predicted to be the world's richest countries in the coming decades.[3] Viet Nam, another example, has seen an extraordinary 210% growth in private wealth over the last decade, driven by its role as an emerging manufacturing hub, and there has also been substantial progress in smaller economies, such as Bangladesh, Mauritius and Tunisia. Dramatic improvements in economic growth, poverty reduction and governance have also taken place even in the world's poorest continent, Africa, over the last decade – sub-Saharan Africa is home to several of the world's fastest growing economies, including Ethiopia, Rwanda and Ghana. By 2030, Asia (excluding Japan) and sub-Saharan Africa could account for approximately 50% of nominal Gross Domestic Product (GDP) worldwide, up from around 20% in 2010, while the contribution of the US, the European Union (EU) and Japan will have halved to around 30%.[4]

Sustained economic growth has meant more money available to governments - as they are able to mobilise more domestic resources for development as well as access private capital markets to pay for their domestic priorities - and to individual consumers to safeguard their needs. This has enabled greater economic independence from the traditionally powerful countries in the West. At the same time, technology has continued to improve, reducing the cost of e.g. life-saving and life-enhancing health interventions. Rising wealth also means Southern countries are exercising more influence at the regional and global levels, playing a bigger part in global solidarity and development efforts, and investing their growing financial resources abroad. In 2012, Southern countries held 46% of global savings and that share is predicted to rise to 62%[5] by 2030, implying that future foreign spending (whether public, private or "blended") will also mostly emanate from the Global South.

This historic shift in income and wealth, which has been progressing for decades, was further boosted by the economic crash in the late 2000s, from which much of the Global South rebounded much more quickly than most high-income economies, some of which continue to experience severe economic difficulties. It represents a dramatic rebalancing of global economic power – and independence – and is challenging dominant economic paradigms, as the "Beijing Consensus" begins to look more attractive to many leaders than an outdated "Washington Consensus". It seems inevitable that the world our grandchildren inherit will be shaped by decisions made in Delhi and Jakarta as much as in London or Paris. Naturally, the traditionally powerful ("Northern" or "Western") countries of the world are demonstrating a more competitive spirit in response. Whereas once countries like China and India (still home to millions of very poor people) would have been treated as requiring support, they are now considered competitors. It is unclear what impact the Covid-19 crisis will have on this dynamic, but there is no reason to suppose that this long-term trend will be reversed.

More contributors, more contributions

These shifts in income, wealth and power affect what different countries now need in terms of international support, financial and otherwise, and what they themselves are able to contribute. The conventional understanding, which has held firm since the 1940s, is that aid is a transfer of resources from rich countries to poor ones. It would be absurd, according to this theory, for poor countries themselves to "give aid". But this is exactly what we are seeing more and more around the world. South-South Cooperation has existed as long as "aid" (perhaps longer) but has increased in prominence over the last two decades. It's not just their financial contributions that are making a difference; policy, research and technology transfer can be as important as money.[6] Many governments offer partnerships that bundle concessional finance with other types of investment, trade, technology and technical assistance. The mix of financial assistance varies from country to country, but loans (both concessional and non-concessional) are common. SSC also emphasises a "double dividend", supporting the development of technical and institutional capabilities in both recipient and contributor country, learning from other countries that have faced the same problems in similar contexts. In these cases, technical assistance provided by low- and middle-income countries may be more appropriate and cheaper than that offered by "traditional" donors.

While ODA has begun to stagnate in recent years, if you add in all the concessional finance and non-monetised SSC from non-OECD countries, **Global Public Investment** overall is probably at an all-time high. South-sourced financial cooperation has increased dramatically since the turn of the millennium, estimated by the OECD now at over US$25 billion per year - almost certainly a low-end estimate, as these estimates do not include all SSC contributors. China is the most talked about Southern contributor. Its Belt and Road Initiative involves massive state-funded investments in infrastructure development across diverse countries in Asia, Europe and Africa.[7] China has pledged to provide Africa with over US$1 trillion in financing by 2025 through direct investment, concessional and commercial loans.[8] China has even bought or invested in European assets worth over

US$300 billion over the last decade, despite European living standards being far higher.[9]

But China is very far from alone. Arab contributors have become particularly prominent with the United Arab Emirates posting some of the highest contributions of any country as a percentage of GNI. It has become something of a badge of honour to open your own aid agency these days, from Kazakhstan to South Africa.[10] Mexico created AMEXCID in 2011,[11] while Turkey's development cooperation agency, TIKA, expanded its budget fifteen-fold between 2002 and 2012.[12] Latin America is particularly vibrant when it comes to SSC, with most countries in the region having international cooperation agencies to support development in neighbouring countries, often by provision of skilled experts.[13] During its boom years, Venezuela was an important partner to Latin American and Caribbean nations especially with its "Petro Caribe" initiative, a lending scheme allowing Caribbean countries to buy Venezuelan oil on extremely preferential terms. It is estimated that Venezuela supplied about US$28 billion in financing this way between 2005 and 2014.[14] Brazil has also been a keen contributor of cooperation, with Brazilian technology to distribute breast milk to help premature babies being shared via government programmes not only in poorer countries like Mozambique and Ghana, but even with wealthy countries like Spain and Portugal.

But it is not just the relatively better off "middle-income" countries that are contributing to international development. The poorest countries are too. India, while a huge economy and one of the BRICS, is still one of the world's poorest countries in per capita terms (somewhat poorer than Djibouti and Nigeria), but its concessional international spending is now probably at least double the aid it receives from traditional donors (roughly US$1.3 billion in expenditures versus US$655 million in receipts in 2014–2015).[15] Bhutan, Ghana, Sri Lanka and Sudan were among India's top ten recipients as far back as 2005-2010 – all have higher per capita incomes than India. Much smaller countries than India have been putting money into global development and solidarity for decades. Countries such as Benin and Zimbabwe have committed millions of dollars to the Global Fund – some of the poorest countries in the world, turned aid "donor". Zambia's pledge of US$5.5 million to the Global Fund's 2019 replenishment, for example, was significantly greater as a proportion of its GNI than "donor" countries such as Belgium. And outside the world of health, Uganda spends around US$300 million per year helping refugees from neighbouring countries, which is over 1% of its annual income. These costs would count as ODA in an OECD country. By that measure, Uganda currently contributes more ODA than any OECD country. All countries, of course, contribute to the UN budget, from large middle-income countries (India contributes about US$20 million per year) to small low-income countries (Mali contributes US$75k). In short, while, on the one hand, the range and depth of development objectives has expanded vastly, so (fortunately) has the range of countries and other partners contributing to a global response.

Extending the principle of universalism

In November 2010, in an article in the Guardian newspaper, I proposed that after the MDGs rather than setting goals for poorer countries which richer countries help achieve, this time, for the first time, wealthy countries should face the same targets.[16] While the problem of extreme poverty is located in the Global South, the problems of inequality and unsustainability are located everywhere. The aspiration should not be only for poorer countries to come up to some standard already demonstrated in richer countries, but for progress in all countries. No longer can we talk about one set of countries that is "developing" versus another that is already "developed". All countries are developing now.

This principle of "universality", as it became known, eventually became the key concept of the SDG era. But what if we apply this vision of universality not just to global targets, but also to the global contributions required to make them a reality? What if, in this SDG era, all countries contribute to global welfare, just as all countries benefit from global progress? Targets for all, financed by all.

The "aid" sector often fails to understand that aid giving is a symbolic act as well as a financial transfer.[17] It enables donors to translate their material dominance into social and moral dominance – not to mention pushing through their economic and political objectives.[18] This is one of the reasons its supposed beneficiaries are so often in two minds about receiving it.[19] By opening up the club of contributors to all countries, power relations would be shifted. The countries that most need development cooperation to work would have their feet more firmly under the table, arguing for their rights and interests from a position of fellow contributor, not just recipient. Countries that have long felt alienated from the foreign aid system, excluded from major decision-making, would be able to engage fully in a new way of working. Encouraging all countries to contribute to efforts to meet global development goals helps cement a paradigm shift in the way we conceive of development, away from charity given by the rich and towards everyone playing their part, no matter how small, for the collective good.

It is politically correct to talk of "partnership" in development circles, but the reality on the ground has too often stuck in the old donor/recipient relationship. In a meaningful partnership, all partners contribute something important. The GPI proposal seeks to make partnership a reality. Obviously, power politics won't just disappear – the biggest players will always exercise their power. But it will be a step-forward, a corrective. It would also, of course, mean more money in the global public pot. According to one recent paper, that considers the impact of extending the 0.7% target to all nations, the financial impact of middle-income countries contributing 0.7% of their GNI to global causes would be significant: about US$150 billion more in additional **Global Public Investment** would become available.[20]

This universalist principle should extend not only to the well-known emerging economies, the so-called middle-income countries, but to *all* countries, including the very poorest. While this might sound radical to some, it is the basis of regional funding mechanisms already, most obviously in the EU (see Chapter 2), and examples of poorer countries making development contributions are already impressively common, as we have seen. The Rwandan government recently donated US$1 million to the Global Fund to Fight AIDS, Tuberculosis and Malaria, becoming the fourth African country to give financial support to the fund. It is a tiny amount compared to the US$700 million the fund has granted to Rwanda, but represents an important intent on behalf of the Rwandan government to be engaged in global development efforts as contributor as well as recipient. The shifting sands of international development should be an opportunity to remake the basis of international financial cooperation. Poorer countries are increasingly keen to capitalise on global power shifts to rejig their place in the world, and are tired of being singled out by development efforts.[21]

Some are concerned that Southern countries will object to the idea of contributing to global development, insisting, rightly, that the Global North has historic and moral obligations to fulfil that cannot be shared out with the Global South.[22] But poor countries would still receive far more than they contribute, and they wouldn't be expected to ramp up contributions overnight. Richer countries would continue to shoulder most of the burden, reflecting their economic circumstances and historic responsibilities. But symbolism can be important: if Liberia, for example, set out gradually to increase its contribution over the next 10 years to, say, US$20 million per annum (far less than it would receive), the world's poorest country would surpass the proportion of GNI currently provided as official development assistance by the US, the world's richest. Importantly, as rich countries quibble about how much they can spare to safeguard the planet and help people leave extreme poverty, far poorer countries would begin to shame richer countries into doing the right thing by allocating a proportion of their severely limited resources for the common good. This proposal does not seek to challenge important historic principles; the Global North will always have larger obligations as part of its responsibility to help redistribute the world's wealth. However, in a changing political context, many in the Global South see an opportunity to engage more fully in global governance and influence the future in a new way.

More recipients, more change

As countries get richer they are better able to target and end extreme poverty, but poverty and inequality continue to exist in all countries, whether in pockets or sometimes just across-the-board. Indeed, far more people live in poverty in so-called middle-income countries (MICs) than in low-income countries (LICs). This raises a tough question for the international community: how to help tackle the persistent exclusion of certain communities and people. It is too simplistic to assume that as countries grow richer, they will provide social and financial protection to their citizens. Some of the Millennium Development Goals may have been achieved *in aggregate terms* in many countries, but there are still populations that are excluded from development progress or are even further marginalised. Development is not a simple function of economic growth, and poverty reduction over the past decades has been neither uniform nor inclusive.[23] Take health. It is now accepted that we need to understand the pockets of health poverty that are found in countries at all income levels: pockets of disease burden (hot spots in concentrated as well as generalised epidemics); pockets of vulnerability (vulnerable populations, young women, refugees, etc.); pockets of gender inequality (structural violence against women, girl-brides, etc.); pockets of injustice or criminalisation (discrimination, human rights violations).

In the health sector there is evidence that vulnerable populations in MICs "graduating" out of ODA are falling between the cracks, that health systems require strengthening and that civil society needs to be supported (including gender and human rights work). With relatively little money, such efforts could be sustained, and countries given more time to adjust and build appropriate responses that might take some decades. Similarly, despite the rhetoric of Universal Health Coverage (UHC), minimal packages are being delivered because of lack of money, and "difficult" diseases such as HIV and TB are left out of UHC plans because there is still vertical funding for them (often from the Global Fund). In the above examples, **GPI** could make a difference, focusing on building both better taxation mechanisms and truly inclusive risk pools to reduce out-of-pocket payments.

If you listen to the common justifications for aid in the aid industry, you would be forgiven for thinking that aid is only useful when it arrives in large quantities to countries in desperate need. But that is only one way concessional IPF is used; the role it plays differs greatly depending on country context. ODA inflows are high only in a fairly small number of countries, mostly very low-income countries and small-island states, where it can account for over 10% of GDP, equivalent to or even higher than the domestic tax take.[24] Most poor people have for some decades lived in countries which rely very little on aid. Very large poor countries (such as India, Nigeria and Indonesia) have never relied on aid, and nor have a whole host of somewhat wealthier, smaller countries, such as those in Latin America. Instead, they have, for many years, received well under 1% of their annual income in external concessional financial support.[25] Even the US Marshall Plan – the United States' aid programme to help rebuild Europe after the Second World War – which is considered large by contemporary standards, and hailed as a great success, was relatively small when inflows are measured as a proportion of recipient GDP. Over the 4 years from 1948 to 1951, the United States transferred US$13 billion (roughly US$115 billion at current prices) to the war-torn nations of Europe, representing about 2% of the collective GDP of European recipient countries.[26]

In fact, the logic that more aid will achieve greater results in poor and fragile countries that are already heavily aid reliant is flawed. Aid has diminishing returns – some of Africa's poorest countries are seeking to reduce aid to emerge from what they recognise as a cycle of dependency. When aid is too large relative to domestic development resources, accountability can be subverted from citizens to donors. Contrary to conventional wisdom in the aid sector, it is precisely where **Global Public Investment** is a relatively small contribution that it can often do the most good.[27] The damaging effects of aid dependency will diminish as the economy grows and aid receipts reduce in relative terms. But, as we have seen in the previous sections, this is no reason to assume that **Global Public Investment** should end entirely when countries pass a certain (arbitrarily set) income per capita threshold. While *dependency* should decline, and while the aid *mentality* needs to evolve, the role of concessional IPF remains important as countries pass the middle-income threshold.

The fact that analyses to date have been predominantly quantitative, without exploring the political and other characteristics of aid versus other types of finance, particularly cumulatively over time, is one of the reasons why issues such as aid dependence and aid conditionality have been allowed to become so harmful. We may be entering a phase in which countries, including the very poorest countries, set out plans to reduce the quantity of **Global Public Investment** they accept in relative terms (i.e. as a proportion of GDP or government spending) while managing an increase in absolute terms as economies continue to grow.

Many countries are thriving on the possibilities of giving as well as receiving support. Colombia's cooperation agency, to take one example, has a directorate for receipts and a directorate for contributions, embodying a modern approach to development cooperation, beyond the binary donor/recipient division. This profoundly challenges traditional understandings of aid. If aid is to fill a financing gap, why would countries that still have such a gap be contributing to other countries, especially ones with higher per capita incomes (implying a smaller gap)? Only if concessional IPF is important in its own right, a special type of money uniquely placed to help because of its special qualities (as I explained in the previous chapter). At the heart of the **Global Public Investment** approach is a critique of the arbitrary thresholds and stingy poverty lines used by many in the traditional aid sector. We refute the assertion that when people cross these poverty lines, or countries cross the income thresholds, there is no further role for concessional international public finance. On the contrary, small amounts of money (relative to the size of the economy) can do a great deal to support development progress.

Covid-19 has highlighted the inadequacy of public services for poorer communities all over the world, in rich countries as well as poorer ones. A new system must ensure that all countries contribute according to capacity, and all benefit according to need. Poorer countries would be net recipients, of course. But poorer regions in richer countries could also benefit directly – where basic health needs for many at present go unmet because governments feel they are limited in the public spending commitments they can make: a problem only sharpened since the 2007/8 financial and Covid-19 health crises. Again, while this sounds radical, it is already happening. According to Japan's Ministry of Foreign Affairs, 163 countries around the world offered financial and technical assistance to Japan following the 2011

Tōhoku earthquake and tsunami. These included many MICs and LICs. For example, Azerbaijan donated US$1 million to the effort, Indonesia US$2 million, Philippines US$10 million, with many more such as Bangladesh, Mexico and others providing experienced search and rescue personnel. The Maldives sent food aid - canned tuna worth almost US$100,000. The Solomon Islands was one of many poorer countries which offered help to Australia in the 2019 wildfires; another was Vanuatu. It is worth reflecting that as Italy endured its worst days of the Covid-19 crisis, countries with much lower incomes per capita – including Cuba, China and Albania – lined up to send help. Doctors without Borders, an NGO, sent a support team to the US in May 2020 to help the Navajo people respond to the Covid-19 crisis.[28]

From graduation to gradation

The international development community is still working out the implications of supporting progress in a world in which the majority of countries are now described as "middle-income", making it questionable how useful the categorisation can be even in simple mathematical terms. The gradual transition of recipient countries out of aid remains a key objective for most bilateral donors. As such, when countries move from low-income to middle-income status the terms of access to concessional IPF change, as countries "graduate" to more expensive forms of finance. For example, eligibility for concessional assistance from the World Bank (through its IDA window) is determined by a country's income per capita (it must be at or below US$1,025 as of 2020), and most traditional ODA donors follow some kind of similar model. Martin Ravallion, a former director of development research at the World Bank, has described the thresholds as "arcane" and called for their removal. Given the host of challenges the world will face in the coming years, we need a more appropriate means of allocating **Global Public Investment** recognising that different types of finance will be appropriate for different countries, not necessarily in a linear way corresponding to income per capita. A range of other categories may be needed to help the aid community in its allocation and effectiveness decisions. There are already exceptions to strict GDP-based rules; for instance, several small islands retain access to concessional World Bank resources despite higher per capita income levels due to their lack of creditworthiness and inherent economic vulnerabilities.

Yes, we should always prioritise the poorest. But often this sensible prioritisation is confused with a needs analysis. In other words, people confuse not needing so much so urgently, with not needing anything at all. The language of dollar-a-day poverty and LICs/MICs/HICs, while sometimes useful, has skewed our understanding of what constitutes need and poverty. It is not that money should be directed away from LICs and towards MICs, but rather that the poverty, inequality and sustainability needs in MICs must be recognised, as well as the role **Global Public Investment** can play in responding to them. Many countries have expressed concern that passing an arbitrary income per capita line has jeopardised their ability to access concessional international public finance despite the fact that they are still unable to access significant amounts of private capital because their economies are considered to be developing.

As we have seen, the simple distinctions between "developed" and "developing", and low, middle and high income, have been replaced with a more nuanced and complex range of development situations. As the number of countries "in the middle" expands further, income per capita will become a less reliable indicator of different countries' specific situations and needs. Under a **Global Public Investment** approach, countries will not *graduate*, rather their receipts will be *gradated* according to their specific needs.[29] Many factors would be considered in assessments of country need. In a paper some of us wrote a few years ago, we suggested, by way of example, three possible criteria: access to credit constraints, space for redistributive policies and environmental vulnerability.[30] This idea is increasingly recognised and is in line with approaches which seek to erode the distinction between LICs and MICs and move beyond GNI as the main (and sometimes only) measure of a countries need for support[31] – the EU, for example, takes into account environmental factors in its formula.

Let's look at one country as an example: South Africa. Since the end of apartheid, the South African government has made remarkable development progress – including setting up inclusive democratic institutions for people of all skin colours, a huge increase in the provision of basic education, healthcare, sanitation and housing and the creation of about millions of jobs. When looking purely at income levels, South Africa averages out not only as middle-income (which it has been for decades, including during apartheid), but as an upper-middle-income country. However, as we have seen, using average income as a proxy for development and, consequently, the need for external assistance, is problematic. The entrenched divisions established under apartheid rendered South Africa one of the most unequal countries in the world, and it is now significantly more unequal almost 30 years after the end of institutionalised racism. Almost 20% of South Africans live below the $1.90 per day poverty, while over half of the population is under the $5.50 per day line. Over 20% of the adult population (15–49 years old) is tragically HIV positive, while almost 30% are unemployed. These worrying statistics have worsened in recent years.[32]

The aid that South Africa receives makes up less than 1% of government expenditure, and about 0.3% of national income, about the same as the early 1990s – South Africa has always funded the vast majority of its own development. Perhaps that is why British officials assumed there would be little outcry when, a few years ago, they announced cuts as part of a strategy to reduce the number of countries supported financially by the UK's Department for International Development (DfID).[33] But when the UK ended its bilateral, grant-based aid programme to South Africa in 2015 it came as an unwelcome shock to the South African government, which vocally expressed its concern. Why? Because even though small, the role of ODA in South Africa was and is important.

Grant assistance has three main roles in South Africa.[34] First, it plays a piloting role, funding relatively small projects that help the government to innovate and improve the delivery of essential basic services. The government can take over successful pilots. The schools' infrastructure support programme, for example, provided millions of dollars to improve schools – including providing furniture, water and electricity – in three of South Africa's poorest regions (Eastern Cape, KwaZulu-Natal and Limpopo), affecting the lives of about 100,000 students. The EU provided €34 million in financial and technical support to improve services – roads, water and energy infrastructure – in KwaZulu-Natal, to support rural development. Both of these initiatives have now been taken over by the government. Second, in addition to directly funding development, the international cooperation community provides a platform for bringing together national and international players that incentivises dialogue and helps share skills and knowledge. As a South African government spokesman aptly pointed out, stopping aid "is tantamount to redefining our relationship" and will affect bilateral relations. Third, aside from assisting the government, aid plays a crucial role in supporting civil society organisations (CSOs) in South Africa, where funding may not be available from domestic sources. South African civil society developed as a powerful force for change during apartheid and continues to play an essential role in human rights activities and service delivery. Funding to CSOs has dwindled since the end of the apartheid, as aid was diverted to the new democratic government.

It's already happening

Some argue that middle-income countries like South Africa can now "pay their own way". If economies grow, and that growth is relatively balanced, household incomes will improve and domestic revenue collection will likely increase. Meanwhile, private investment from abroad will be attracted by better opportunities and improving infrastructure. This correct generalisation has led the international community to a point whereby when countries pass a certain income per capita threshold it is assumed official foreign assistance should decline over time and eventually end entirely. There are three problems with this argument. First, as we have seen, the need in these countries is far greater than usually assumed. Because some countries need help *more* than others, those others are deemed not to need help *at all*. Strategically prioritising scarce resources towards the very poorest countries should not be mistaken for a serious needs analysis of slightly less poor countries. The "bottom billion" approach to aid allocation, focusing interventions on fragile states and questioning the role of international cooperation in MICs,[35] makes some sense if funds are strictly limited; so as well as the debate about how to cut the cake, we need to maintain the debate about the *size* of that cake, to respond to continued poverty and sustainability needs in MICs.

The second major problem with the assertion that MICs no longer need financial support is that it is over-optimistic regarding the political feasibility of wealth and income redistribution. It is to be welcomed that more and more government and international analysts (including the OECD and the IMF) are emphasising the problems of intra-country inequality and the crucial redistributive role of taxation, picking up on the work done for decades by civil society and academics. Whether we are living in a new era of global inequality or simply noticing it more is not the point; deep inequality is entrenched in most countries and has been for centuries. Trying to persuade the haves to share wealth and opportunities more generously with the have-nots is at the heart of any political struggle. But when it comes to discussing the rising incomes of poorer countries, especially as they cross the arbitrary middle-income boundary, many analysts imply that fairer redistribution of growing wealth is possible and even likely in a reasonably short space of time, say 5 or 10 years. There is little evidence for such optimism, bar a revolution. The likelihood of significant change in a short timeframe is close to zero – certainly not entrenched, irreversible, change. Generally, such shifts take decades at least – quite a different timeframe than that envisaged in most aid transition periods. Take India. You might assume it is a hugely unequal country, and it is. But, like many Southern countries, it has a Gini coefficient on a par with most Northern countries, and significantly below that of the US – meaning that income distribution is fairer in India than in the US. Given the stubborn reality of deep inequalities over the centuries, and the fact that in many countries they are getting worse, donor confidence that they will be able to exit without jeopardising the well-being of many millions of poor people is open to serious question.

The third problem is that, as we established in Chapter 4, it is a misconception that international public money can simply be replaced by other types of money, most obviously domestic public investment but also private spending. According to such an analysis, aid is considered something of a last resort, still being made available to those countries which have severely limited access either to domestic or private financial options, but eventually to be phased out as such countries become an even rarer phenomenon. But **Global Public Investment** is not simply a stop-gap, it is a unique source of funding whose characteristics make it well-qualified to play a significant pro-development role in a range of countries, including MICs and even high-income countries (HICs). While it is certainly welcome that most countries are moving on from *dependence* on aid, the continued availability of **Global Public Investment** needs to remain a central plank of the overall development finance offer.

Another objection sometimes raised is that money from abroad reduces national pressure for change, the so-called "moral hazard" argument. In some instances, international interference may lessen political pressure for pro-poor changes, but this objection could be made for any country, low- or middle-income, and there is a strong argument that as **Global Public Investment** diminishes as a proportion of the economy, it is less likely to dissuade redistributive measures (it is not big enough to have such an effect) but could promote such measures, through good example and targeted interventions.

Development cooperation is evolving away from a sometimes patronising exercise in supporting countries poorer than one's own, into a permanent feature on the global map in which a host of new and possibly surprising relationships are emerging. While it is inevitable that the richer countries shoulder most of the burden, it is plausible that in the near future all countries will contribute something substantial to international development cooperation efforts. The involvement of even the poorest countries will be important for what it signifies – that this is a global effort involving all countries not just a few, and that all countries should take part in decision-making. Moves in this direction are already underway.

There has always been a wide variety of organisations engaged in development cooperation; one analysis counted at least 400 separate intergovernmental entities supporting international cooperation established between 1930 and 2004.[36] And during the MDG era that variety blossomed to new levels, in part because of geopolitical changes, and in part also because of the emphasis the UN and others laid on partnerships to achieve the MDGs. Advances in technology have made international cooperation between different actors and across borders easier as well. While previous eras saw contributions dominated by rich country governments the present context is far more sophisticated. Many countries are already both contributing and receiving development cooperation, which is now a more complex web of interaction and mutual solidarity and interest than the traditional donor/recipient story.

Countries can benefit from **Global Public Investment** long after they become "middle-income", that randomly conferred status beloved of the aid industry. Of course, as countries move up the income scale, the need for foreign public inflows evolves and other options open up for supporting poverty reduction, equality and sustainable development. But concessional finance can still be effectively invested in countries well up the income scale, depending on their particular circumstances. As we have seen, it is not just valuable when it is large-scale, filling budgetary gaps; it can be an important pro-development intervention even in these "low aid" countries, as a small proportion of GNI, catalysing change and overcoming blockages and traps. The EU is perhaps the best-known example of this, where large amounts of concessional funds have been redistributed to upper-middle and high-income countries for the last few decades.[37]

The paradigm shifts outlined in this chapter may seem radical at first but are in fact already apparent. Much of what we are saying is just a better description of the changing reality of international development cooperation. We now need to talk about what kind of governance changes might be possible to help manage what is an increasingly complex array of interests and interventions.

Notes

1. Colombia, Indonesia, Vietnam, Egypt, Turkey, and South Africa.
2. Bangladesh, Egypt, Indonesia, Iran, Mexico, Nigeria, Pakistan, Philippines, South Korea, Turkey and Vietnam.
3. https://www.reuters.com/article/emerging-economies-2050-idAFL6-E8CB55620120111.
4. UNDP HDR, 2013. Estimates made before the Covid-19 crisis.

5. https://www.worldbank.org/en/news/feature/2013/05/15/developing-countries-to-dominate-global-saving-and-investment-but-the-poor-will-not-necessarily-share-the-benefits-says-report

6. UNCTAD, Trade and Development Report 2015: http://unctad.org/en/PublicationsLibrary/tdr2015_en.pdf.

7. See this article in the Guardian: https://www.theguardian.com/cities/ng-interactive/2018/jul/30/what-china-belt-road-initiative-silk-road-explainer.

8. Yun (2014).

9. See Bloomberg figures: https://www.bloomberg.com/graphics/2018-china-business-in-europe/.

10. https://www.devex.com/news/waiting-for-south-africa-s-new-aid-agency-82369.

11. https://www.gob.mx/amexcid.

12. http://www.tika.gov.tr/en/.

13. See the website of the Ibero-American General Secretariat for more information: https://www.segib.org/en/ibero-american-cooperation/south-south-cooperation/.

14. SELA, 2015 and http://www.huffingtonpost.com/otaviano-canuto/oil-prices-and-the-future_b_8209010.html.

15. See this article in Devex: www.devex.com/news/in-latest-indian-budget-aid-spending-dwarfs-aid-receipts-82915.

16. https://www.theguardian.com/global-development/poverty-matters/2010/nov/03/millennium-development-goals-inequality

17. See Hattori, T. (2001): https://www.jstor.org/stable/4177404?seq=1.

18. https://www.bloomberg.com/news/articles/2013-03-18/its-time-to-reform-usaid.

19. https://www.spiegel.de/international/world/interview-with-rwandan-president-paul-kagame-we-are-far-from-exhausting-our-potential-a-704894.html.

20. Figures from Glennie, Gulrajani, Sumner and Wickstead (2019).

21. Africa was the only continent specifically mentioned in the Millennium Declaration, an indignity it did not suffer in the SDG preamble.

22. This is usually a particularly key argument in UN negotiations led by the G77, and the call for reparations is rising again in various forums.

23. Multiple studies have shown that progress has been faster for the better off than for in the poorest. See for example: UN, Millennium Development Goals Report (2013) and UNICEF, "Social Protection: Accelerating the MDGs with Equity" (2010).

24. European Commission, Beyond 2015: towards a comprehensive and integrated approach to financing povertyeradication and sustainable development(2013): http://ec.europa.eu/transparency/regdoc/rep/1/2013/EN/1-2013-531-EN-F1-1.Pdf.

25. Glennie and Prizzon (2012).

26. Eichengreen Barry, Lessons from the Marshall Plan, 2010: http://web.worldbank.org/archive/website01306/web/pdf/wdr_2011_case_study_marshall_plan_1.pdf.

27. https://www.odi.org/publications/6383-high-low-aid-proposal-classify-countries-aid-receipt.

28. https://www.cbsnews.com/news/doctors-without-borders-navajo-nation-coronavirus/.
29. Sagasti et al. referenced in Glennie and Hurley (2014a).
30. Alonso et al. (2014).
31. Gaspar et al. (2019).
32. All stats from WDI.
33. At the time the UK was the country's third largest "donor" (after the US and the EU).
34. Analysis and statistics from https://www.odi.org/publications/7392-eu-development-policy-aid-middle-income-countries-mics-differentiation-south-africa.
35. As proposed by Paul Collier in his influential book "The Bottom Billion" in 2007.
36. Kaul and Conceição (2006)
37. Glennie and Hurley (2014b).

6 GOVERNANCE
From hierarchical to horizontal

- *Traditional analysis*: **Foreign aid** is spent on an *ad hoc* basis, with key decisions made by a small group of countries.

- *New paradigm*: **Global Public Investment** should be overseen more democratically, through processes that respond better to today's geopolitics and include civil society.

We have seen that we need to raise our ambition for what can be achieved with international public funds, that we need to renew our understanding of how it operates relative to other sources of finance, and that we need to move on from old-fashioned notions of donor/recipient. But how should this new approach be managed, or to use the jargon, *governed*? If we are serious about asking all countries to contribute, how should decisions be taken on how the money is spent? In short, how can the hundreds of billions of dollars in **Global Public Investment** be invested more effectively and accountably than foreign aid has been? To answer those questions, we first need to look at how GOVERNANCE of the aid ecosystem works at the moment, and then see what aspects are ripe for change.

The trouble with aid

"For all the sophistication of the modern global economy and the speed with which it can conduct commerce, the architecture to deal with problems of the public realm and collective responsibility remain sorely underdeveloped. Part of the problem stems from a hopelessly inefficient and inadequate method of funding international collective action, which relies on hat-passing and pledges from nations that are either not forthcoming or, if they are, are frequently never met".
Andrew Simms, Fellow at the New Economics Foundation[1]

Aid has had many successes. Most often cited by aid enthusiasts are large-scale vaccination programmes, emergency relief and less tangible outcomes such as the impact over time of support for women's rights. However, there is also a large body of work critiquing aid for ineffectiveness and, at times, actually causing a negative impact, whether immediately or cumulatively over time.

On the recipient side, a lack of institutional capacity and corruption are some of the reasons for poor performance. On the contributor side, the usual problems are things like a lack of local knowledge, poor alignment with national development priorities, short-term project cycles (versus long-term development needs) and poor coordination between aid providers. High transaction costs are also problematic – it is time-consuming for recipient country institutions to coordinate and report on high quantities of aid, especially when it comes from multiple providers. There are also problems associated with aid dependence, most notably the conditions donors have tended to attach to aid, known as "conditionalities", usually reflecting certain political ideologies. The 1980s saw a marked increase in the use of donor and lender conditionality, reaching into the minutiae of national policy such as taxation and expenditure plans.[2] For instance, in the late 1990s the IMF intervened in the Asian financial crisis with a series of billion-dollar bailouts to help the economies of Southeast Asia avoid default. As part of the deal, which countries in deep economic distress could hardly refuse, it imposed severe and controversial policy conditionalities, many of which were not needed to manage the crisis, such as financial liberalisation and spending cuts.[3] The IMF was heavily criticised for its failure to adequately consider the social impact of their ideas, especially on public services and unemployment. Clearly the bailouts were needed, and clearly some conditions must accompany major loans of any kind. The question is: who sets the conditions? The institutional framework within which international public finance is mediated should be reformed; accountability and decision-making in particular need a good dose of democracy. The IMF still attaches on average 20 conditions to its loans. Recent loans to Cyprus, Greece and Jamaica have contained an average 35 conditions including on public sector reform, trade liberalisation and privatisation of major state-owned enterprises. Sources suggest that in the middle of the Covid-19 crisis, with countries in the Global South desperate for emergency cash, the World Bank (led by Donald Trump's ally David Malpass) has been using the opportunity to attach ideological conditions to its loans, effectively blackmailing poor countries.[4]

Understanding the mixed motives behind aid helps explain its mixed record. Though often well-intentioned and almost always accompanied by altruistic rhetoric, aid has also served a wide range of economic, political, moral and cultural objectives for provider nations, from securing trade advantages to building political alliances. For instance, John F. Kennedy's Alliance for Progress, launched in 1961, aimed to accelerate the economic and social development of Latin America, but the programme was also motivated by a desire to inhibit the rise of communism in the region. According to one typical analysis, "an inefficient, economically closed, mismanaged non-democratic former colony politically friendly to its former colonizer, receives more foreign aid than another country with similar level of poverty, a superior policy stance, but without a past as a colony".[5] Direct commercial interests have also influenced foreign spending, with much aid being "tied" to the purchase of specific commodities and services, with a small number of countries receiving the majority of ODA.[6] The balance between geopolitical, historical and commercial interests versus development motives varies between donors but most studies conclude that contributor self-interest is an important determinant that helps explain aid quantities and destination. One study carried out at the height of the MDG campaign estimated that only one-third of aid allocation is driven by recipient need.[7] Donors' mixed motivations for aid also help to explain why promises – such as the one to allocate between 0.15 and 0.2% of GNI to the Least Developed Countries (LDCs) – are not met by most donors.

While this book is calling for a ramping up of **Global Public Investment** for sustainable development, we must be under no illusions about the complex impacts of international interventions. Some people use these challenges as an excuse to call for an end to foreign assistance. But the fact that it is hard to get it right doesn't mean we should just give up. When money is misspent at the national level – and corruption in public financial management is a major issue in most countries around the world – we don't call for an end to public spending! Countries need to increase tax take and public spending if they are to achieve public goods, even though there are great challenges. It is the same internationally.

By recognising where aid has gone wrong in the past, we can build a better governance structure for **Global Public Investment**. Politics and the quest for national advantage are not going anywhere, so the perennial problems associated with aid and other types of international public money are not going to disappear. As we call for reform we must also set ourselves realistic ambitions. Some attempts have been made to improve the way aid works, but they have largely been technocratic and have failed to get to the heart of the problem, which is political. For instance, the Paris aid effectiveness principles sought to increase aid's positive impact through improved alignment with local development priorities, better coordination between donors and a focus on development results.[8] But the political and bureaucratic incentives within donor organisations are only marginally influenced by statements of intent at an international level, and the instincts of politicians and their accountants to achieve short-term results and avoid risky investments have undermined attempts to improve aid effectiveness in the long term.

These realities make the aid system incredibly slow to respond to promises and commitments. The OECD and UNDP reported in 2019 that longstanding efforts to change the way development aid is delivered so that it is more transparent, predictable and "country-owned" (rather than driven by donor priorities) were being met with mixed success at best.[9] Furthermore, just when some governments do begin to respond to commitments, they sometimes suddenly go out of fashion, seemingly passé, as the context changes and new priorities are set – the aid effectiveness agenda of just 10 years ago is now considered ancient history by many in the aid sector.[10]

Political commitment to international processes on aid effectiveness remains mixed and aid allocation decisions continue to be made by donors on an individualised basis rather than in close coordination. Uncoordinated supply-driven aid remains a major problem and donors remain reluctant to channel resources through recipient countries' national systems despite promises to do so. Despite a recent proliferation in multilateral funds specialised in areas such as health and climate, donors continue to display a preference for bilateral aid channels. Ultimately, when you hold the purse strings you determine how and where the money will be spent – as well as the conditions under which it will be supplied, but governance reform at the Bretton Woods institutions like the World Bank and the IMF, at which a few historically powerful countries have a veto over decision-making, has also stalled. These ongoing problems demonstrate the limitations of "technical" fixes to issues which are more political in nature. Nevertheless, the problems associated with aid and the factors that contribute to its success (or otherwise) in one context versus another are at least now much better acknowledged and understood. The new paradigm proposed in this book, and the upheaval and out-of-box thinking brought about by Covid-19, presents a perfect opportunity to update and improve the structures and institutions that have governed aid for the past 60 years. As well as addressing technical barriers, we also need (finally) to address the institutions that manage international cooperation.

From OECD to UN

In 1970, the UN General Assembly agreed that "economically advanced countries" should make efforts to provide 0.7% of GNI as ODA, a term which quickly became synonymous with aid. The idea was that aid providers should achieve the 0.7% target by the mid-1970s, but 50 years later few countries have met it (although they all dutifully repeat their commitment in regular international meetings). But that was as far as the UN got in terms of managing this resource. It was the OECD, and its Development Assistance Committee (DAC), that retained control of what should count as ODA and how it should be spent, even though many countries, from the USSR to China to the Arab states, have long provided very large quantities of concessional international public finance without coming under the OECD's purview.

Since 1972, the OECD DAC has defined ODA as those flows which have "the promotion of the economic development and welfare of developing countries" as the main objective and which are "concessional in character".[11] This definition is broad enough to have attracted much criticism, from whether debt cancellation and the domestic costs of educating students from the Global South should count as aid, to whether new priorities such as climate change adaptation and mitigation should be managed separately from aid budgets. Recently, as market interest rates have reduced, doubts have been raised about the "concessionality" of loans described as aid that are actually returning a significant margin to the lending country.

Furthermore, this definition is far from universal, an increasingly important disjuncture as the actors involved in international public financing continue to increase. Non-OECD donors have no standard definition and are free to define their interventions as they choose. South-South Cooperation is considered a manifestation of solidarity among people and countries of the Global South that contributes to their national well-being, their national and collective self-reliance and the attainment of internationally agreed development goals. As such, South-South Cooperation is guided by a loose set of the principles specific to this type of cooperation.

The emergence of new bilateral contributors to the pot and the re-emergence in force of other longstanding non-OECD contributors such as China and India have added to the complexity of the global public finance landscape, increased the amount of support available and thrown into sharp relief the complex motives and objectives of international public finance; like everyone else, these South-South contributors are motivated by a combination of humane concern and strategic benefit. It is absurd, in 2020, for a small club of rich countries to maintain power over what aid means, and how it should be prioritised and otherwise managed. Understandably, the OECD is worried about a world in which the power of its members seems to be ebbing, and it is keen to keep hold of the levers of power that it does still control. But it won't work, and this is as good a time as any to move things forward. Economic resurgence has been accompanied by major shifts in geopolitical power and influence. Countries in the Global South are increasingly insisting on their right to contribute to the rules that dominate global trade, finance and investment. This implies that, in addition to being accountable to their main shareholders, international financial institutions should also be accountable to their borrowers.

Controlling the definition of ODA means OECD members states control the direction in which it is heading. While broad and open to interpretation, it reflects the interests and objectives of OECD members. The focus on poverty, for example, which was pushed for by OECD countries, is understandable but limited. Many Southern countries asked whether the heavy prioritisation on supporting primary schooling was the right one given the need for well-educated high school graduates and indeed PhDs to build industrial economies. Discussions are underway about widening the criteria for what "counts" as aid to provide, for example, more in the form of loans on market terms, for international security purposes or to relax tied aid rules.[12] Whatever the merits of these debates, they should be happening in open global forums, organised by the UN, not the club of rich countries.

Tussles over how development aid is "counted" are another indicator of the challenges associated with raising resources for spending beyond national borders. Donors have an incentive to count as many expenditures as they can as aid, including those that benefit primarily domestic companies or individuals, as well as resources that stay in the provider nation and offer dubious benefit to Southern countries. For example, OECD donor countries count some expenditures associated with domestic "development education" programmes as well as in-donor country refugee costs as development aid, a policy decried as "phantom aid" by many NGOs. OECD members can do this because they themselves determine what counts as aid and what does not. It is increasingly important that the growing contributions of non-OECD countries are tracked and managed better to ensure high-quality impacts. But this continuing breach between OECD countries and others is hindering a coherent framework to do so. Most emerging economies do not describe their interventions as "aid" and understandably do not want to be governed by OECD strictures.[13]

Attributes of effective governance

The landscape of international public spending is more complex, interesting and diverse than ever before, from the variety of countries and institutions now involved, to the broad range of issues tackled, to the financing approaches and technologies employed. And it is still changing fast. These changes make spending more difficult to analyse, and indeed much of this expenditure is poorly scrutinised. Yet these are *public* resources and accountability for how and where they are used is critical. The need to build more inclusive partnerships between all those involved is the critical element of governance reform, and that means clearer focus on voice, accountability, representation and ownership.

A longstanding concern of the countries of the Global South and advocacy groups has been the asymmetry of representation and voice in decisions regarding the financial and development policies and practices of the World Bank, the IMF, bilateral agencies and the Paris Club of official creditors. An effective **Global Public Investment** architecture should give *voice* to all relevant stakeholders. The South-South Cooperation movement gathers together many different models of cooperation, but one theme threaded through it is an emphasis on greater recipient ownership, based on a philosophy of "horizontality". The simple existence of a larger range of possible cooperation partners has increased recipients' room for manoeuvre and their bargaining power in the international arena. An effective **GPI** architecture would allocate funds based on recipient country need and performance, tailoring financial instruments and institutional arrangements to specific conditions. While accountability is the central governance concern, from which all else falls into place, we also propose the following principles for effective governance of **Global Public Investment**.[14]

- *Adequacy.* While quantity is not the be-all and end-all – because the qualities of **GPI** make it important even at low levels – clearly there does need to be adequate public money at the international level to respond to the scale of global threat and the ambition of the SDGs to build a better, fairer world. There are many ways to estimate the quantity required, but it is clear that we are talking about an order of magnitude far greater than what is currently available.

- *Efficiency.* Institutional, administrative and transaction costs should be reasonably low, without being reduced to the point where the ability to plan, manage, coordinate and engage in meaningful dialogue is impaired.
- *Predictability.* The lack of predictability in financial flows to recipient countries creates significant problems for macro-economic management, public expenditure planning and institutional development, and may also undermine the confidence of private investors. If you make commitments, you should see them through. On time.
- *Diversity.* A wide range of instruments will be required to meet the large variety of global needs, tailored to specific recipient situations, including a country's capacity to mobilise external and domestic resources. We will need to balance letting "a thousand flowers bloom" to allow for creativity and an element of competition, with some kind of order to ensure every part of the system pulls its weight and is overseen appropriately.
- *Responsiveness.* This refers to the capacity of the **Global Public Investment** architecture to respond rapidly and effectively to external shocks – health crises, financial crises, violent conflicts, natural disasters, sudden surges and collapses of commodity prices – and, if possible, anticipate them.
- *Flexibility and learning.* An effective **Global Public Investment** architecture needs to be flexible in a context of changing need and context. This should include the possibility of closing or merging organisations that have outlived their usefulness, and, where justified, the establishment of new ones. Management procedures and incentives should be structured to foster innovation and judicious risk taking, and also to learn from past failures and the mistakes of others.
- *Complementarity.* External sources of finance should be seen as a complement to domestic resources and, as such, they should help create the institutional framework, policy environment and habits that promote domestic savings and investment, both public and private.

New technologies could play a role in enhancing accountability. The fundamental change offered by mobile technology, and the reason it could help embed a new generation of **Global Public Investment**, is the potential to provide an infrastructure for demand-driven, transparent and direct exchange, with low transaction costs. Mobile technology makes inclusion and exchange easier and cheaper; it can empower people and deliver abundant data that can be used in the public interest. Digital health, for example, has the potential to revolutionise the way healthcare services are provided and financed. It can help run services more efficiently, transparently and inclusively, empowering people to be agents of services as opposed to merely recipients of care. Private mobile wallets can help build large risk pools, manage financial transactions from multiple funding sources (personal, public, private), monitor actual payments and use of services and manage quality control against marginal costs. At the same time, there are substantial risks with new technologies, including of data and privacy abuse by both governments, corporations and others. The major effort required to achieve the potential benefits of new technologies will only be possible when countries work in partnership to introduce appropriate public regulation.

From top-down to bottom-up

The **Global Public Investment** approach insists that financing global goods should not be left to the vagaries of charity or the private sector, but that nation states should lead the way with formal, monitored contributions. However, it does not follow that other stakeholders should be excluded from decision-making processes. It is no longer sufficient, if it ever was, to suggest that national governments are the only legitimate entities to govern global development efforts, even when they are the major contributors of finance. A much wider range of stakeholders is increasingly being recognised as critical to ensure the effectiveness and accountability of development interventions. Among those stakeholders, and high up the list of priorities, is civil society. Civil society should be included in decision-making processes at all levels, to facilitate citizen-led monitoring of progress and adherence to commitments. Strengthening social-led accountability is necessary to maintain the integrity of the public sector, prevent corruption-related resource drain, and ensure more appropriate and sustainable public programs.

Civil society has played a central role in global development progress over the past 20 years, through advocacy and service delivery. Human rights advocacy remains crucial to promote global equality and to achieve SDG targets, giving people a voice in the decisions that affect their lives and holding governments accountable for meeting the needs of all people, including marginalised groups. It plays a key role in building strong systems for health, education, economic opportunity, upholding the rule of law and protecting human rights. Policies developed with broad participation that include civil society help governments and institutions provide better services. Advocates detect problems and raise awareness, participate in policy dialogue, contribute to designing policy solutions and marshal support to adopt them. But the work of civil society doesn't end with the passage of policy measures. Advocacy helps ensure equitable and effective implementation of policies, monitor the impact of those policies, ensure quality of service delivery and identify continuing challenges. Civil society is often best placed to gain access to, represent, and prioritise the most marginalised key populations, and advocacy is needed to support resource mobilisation, reducing out of pocket expenses and achieving the aims of the SDGs. Advocates push national governments to progressively increase their investment in public services and infrastructure and push the international community to provide funding in alignment with countries' plans, helping countries in the Global South bridge significant finance gaps. Civil society, in short, gives people a voice in the decisions that affect their lives and helps hold governments accountable for meeting the needs of all people, including marginalised groups. The role of civil society in service delivery is equally important. Community- and peer-based services enhance service delivery and provide safe spaces for marginalised populations that are often wary of utilising state-based facilities for fear of abuse or discrimination.

Civil society must therefore be included in decision-making and monitoring processes at all levels. Civil society is a term covering a wide range of organisations, from international NGOs wielding very large sums of money to grassroots organisations linking up across borders. Since the 1980s the sector has grown in both number and size, and where once it operated on the periphery of formal development processes, it is now often intimately involved with official actors, either as implementers of government-funded programmes, partners in national, regional or global alliances, or accorded formal oversight roles in internationally negotiated agreements. The Global Fund to Fight AIDS, Tuberculosis and Malaria has spearheaded civil society participation in governance at its Board and Secretariat and at country level. This has led to greater use of evidence and rights-based approaches to care delivery, increased inclusion of marginalised populations in prevention and healthcare services and improved oversight of resource allocation and implementation.

It is worth mentioning that funding for civil society in much of the world is increasingly scarce, and funding for advocacy even more so (most funding is for service delivery and project implementation). At the national level, where the need is greatest, sources of funding are in their infancy, and are often non-existent. National governments are usually reticent to fund groups likely to criticise them; the private sector tends to steer clear of advocacy, preferring more concrete, and less potentially challenging, approaches, and may also often be opposed to the aims of civil society advocacy; the general public is not a major supplier of funds to charitable causes in most countries in the Global South, and often avoids supporting issues that are deemed politically sensitive. This means that civil society advocacy relies heavily on international funding from three major sources: philanthropy (i.e. major foundations), public donations (from the Global North) and ODA. While the contribution of philanthropists and the general public is welcome, it is unacceptably precarious for the crucial work of civil society to be dependent on the (generally quite unaccountable) decisions of a handful of very wealthy people and uncertain charitable funds. The problem faced by many civil society advocates in the Global South today is that ODA money is drying up. As countries "graduate" to "middle-income" status, the OECD donors are pulling their funding. Meanwhile, South-South Cooperation, which is on the increase, tends not to support civil society, preferring direct relationships with governments. Money is not the only ingredient in successful advocacy, but it is a necessary one. As it becomes scarcer, important advocacy programmes, usually seeking to focus attention on key marginalised groups, are under threat. The key attributes of **Global Public Investment** – availability, motivation, concessionality, expertise, accountability – are therefore critical to the continued financing of global civil society.

From voluntary to statutory

Foreign aid is usually considered a voluntary act offered on an *ad hoc* basis as per the autonomy of the Northern donor, but over time **Global Public Investment** should evolve from being voluntary gifts to stable contributions according to an agreed formula, so that key multilateral funds can be replenished, and major crises responded to in an orderly way. The United Nations and related specialised agencies are probably the closest we come to any sort of formalised "system" for international collaboration and the financing of international public policy concerns, such as peace and security, economic development, humanitarian and health emergencies, the conservation and protection of world heritage sites and macroeconomic stability. Even in these cases however, only a portion of UN activities are funded via compulsory (or "assessed") financial contributions. Most of the UN's major funds and programmes are financed through voluntary donations. These include well-known names such as the UNDP and the United Nations Children's Fund (UNICEF), many of which have seen their budgets squeezed over recent years. Donald Trump's decision in May 2020 to not only defund the World Health Organisation, but cut ties to it, demonstrates how precarious these crucial global institutions remain. The African Union is funded in part by assessed contributions from its 54 member countries but a larger share currently comes from international donors who provide funds – in cash or kind – voluntarily. NATO, meanwhile, operates a cost-share formula based on GNI combined with voluntary donations and other *ad hoc* arrangements to support particular programmes.[15] Most of NATO's resources are sourced from member countries' ministries of defence. Interpol is also funded via annual statutory contributions plus additional voluntary contributions in cash or kind.

Even where contributions are supposedly compulsory, countries often fail to pay, with major countries often billions of dollars in arrears. There is little to force countries to pay – beyond appeal to their better nature or exclusion from an association. Decisions not to pay may sometimes be economic but they are more likely to be political. It is not always easy to exclude a member country for their failure to pay (or for other perceived bad behaviour), especially when it is rich or otherwise influential. Enforceability therefore continues to be a difficult issue. The closest we come towards any kind of "mandatory" financial contribution for "international" causes is in the cases where states have established a dedicated organisation which aims to pursue a shared interest. Membership of the entity is voluntary but implies an obligation to contribute to its costs through "assessed contributions" i.e. mandatory fees levied on member countries, in accordance with their ability to pay. The danger, of course, is that relatively wealthier countries have more resources to establish institutions that will address the issues that matter most to them.

A system based on voluntary contributions is utterly inadequate and cannot produce the kinds of social, environmental, security and other outcomes the world needs to see. It is absurd that when disaster strikes a country, for instance, it should have to wait in hope that other countries are feeling generous in their response – there should be permanent funds available, just as there are at the national level, and in some regions e.g. the European Union. And the same goes for other development priorities. An agreed formula could also replace the triennial begging-bowl rounds in which multilateral banks and international financial institutions seek voluntary contributions from their members. While it will be hard to enforce such a system, peer pressure could help it work sufficiently well to be useful – the Central Emergency Response Fund (CERF) and UN membership contributions are examples of where it has already been tried (with mixed results). Countries could still direct their contribution to the objectives and organisations that most tallied with their priorities. Re-modelling the system according to a **Global Public Investment** approach so that all contribute a fair share would help remake the case for global development to sceptical publics, rebalancing the power dynamics that so often taint the dealings of donors and recipients.

From bilateral to multilateral

Over recent years, trust and confidence in old forms of multilateral cooperation has declined, particularly when it is globally (rather than regionally) constituted. Despite growth across the world and the desire of many countries to increase their international assertiveness and contribution, the global bodies have been slow to respond. The Bretton Woods institutions, which mediate and channel international public finance, offer little more than rhetoric when it comes to governance reform and have been heavily criticised for their failure to anticipate financial crises and for sometimes worsening the impacts of those crises where they do occur. Clearly, reform is required.

When it comes to cross-border public financing there continues to be an institutional vacuum and inchoate ideas about governance. For instance, the bulk of financing from the development banks continues to be focused on national public good delivery; regional and cross-border initiatives remain relatively small fry. A dizzying array of initiatives and collaborations now exists in areas such as public health and the environment: from "vaccine" bonds (bonds that raise funds on international capital markets for immunisation programmes in poor countries repaid by donors' future aid budgets), to "cash on delivery" schemes (where payments are tied to results) to highly specialised mixed public and private "vertical" funds (such as the Global Alliance for Vaccines and Immunisation – GAVI – which combines public and private finance and expertise to expand access to vaccines in some of the world's poorest countries). The number of entities that mobilise and channel public (or mixed public and private) resources to international concerns has mushroomed over recent years. The OECD's definition of ODA remains broad, to better reflect donor interests, and OECD donors tend to favour bilateral aid channels, which give them greater influence over how and where funds are used, over multilateral alternatives. The OECD reports that 72% of development aid is delivered bilaterally versus just 28% via multilateral channels.[16]

Global Public Investment would either be bilateral, including to nearby countries – thus building regional ties and supporting regional development – or, more straightforwardly, multilateral, including to major UN initiatives. Poor countries could buy small shares in the development banks, wielding disproportionate shareholder power as campaigners have done recently in major businesses. The shift of power to the Global South has led not only to more states becoming actively involved in the financing of international concerns (because they have both the resources and the incentives to do so) but also the setting up of new multilateral entities to channel their collective financing. This has been driven, in part, by frustration at the failure to adjust the distribution of power in traditional multilateral institutions such as the IMF and World Bank in line with emerging economies' rising economic weight. Many of the world's largest channels for international cooperation and financing were established in the immediate post-Second World War period and their governance arrangements reflect the balance of power prevailing in the world at the time of their creation. For example, the United States holds a 16.7% voting share in the IMF while four European nations hold 17.6%. In contrast, the four "BRIC" economies (Brazil, Russia, India, China) have a combined share of just 10.3%. In 2013, the BRICS nations announced plans to establish a BRICS Development Bank and a joint special reserve fund to support macroeconomic stabilisation.[17] As many countries have found, it's often easier to establish a whole new entity than to reform an old one. But this also presents coordination challenges in what is now a heavily fragmented international cooperation and financing landscape.

Recent years have seen increasing regional integration, politically and economically, often including joint public spending initiatives. Regional development banks have taken on a more prominent role and new innovative forms of regional cooperation have emerged.[18] For instance, the Caribbean Catastrophe Risk Insurance Facility (CCRIF) provides short-term liquidity to Caribbean governments when catastrophic hurricanes and earthquakes strike. It is funded through contributions from major donors as well as membership fees from governments of the region. Regional development institutions rely extensively on international capital markets to fund important shares of their operations. But many also still depend on large and regular contributions from governments, combined with income from loan repayments made overwhelmingly by governments. In the wake of the 2008 financial crisis, regional development banks received extraordinary capital injections far superior to those received by their global counterpart, the World Bank. Like other public multilateral bodies, regional organisations are able to play an important counter-cyclical role. This increased "regionalisation" is good for development prospects in the years ahead. Poverty and sustainability challenges are not confined by national boundaries – there are spill-over effects to neighbouring countries. The strong intra-regional bias that character-ises much international public finance is no accident as these resources can be used to enhance trade and investment opportunities close to home. Security objectives may also be a factor as there can be seri-ous risks associated with a "failed state" or conflict on your doorstep (e.g. violence and instability spilling across the border and/or large numbers of people fleeing conflict or economic hardship). Regional groupings allow for closer and more representative decision-making and increased political and economic cooperation at the regional level can foster greater regional stability. Poorer and smaller countries, which still struggle to secure adequate voice and representation in the international arena, are more likely to be heard in regional groupings. Several emerging economies have founded or proposed new institu-tions for financial and technical collaboration amongst themselves, such as the Asian Infrastructure Investment Bank (AIIB) which sup-ports infrastructure construction in Asia and the Pacific.

Despite the high degree of technical expertise which many agencies have now accumulated, the response of the international community to humanitarian crises is sometimes criticised for its inadequacy and its ineffectiveness. This reflects, in part, the reality that some emergen-cies and disasters receive widespread support while others are poorly publicised and receive little public and political attention. This can translate into a suboptimal response which is often suboptimal. It also reflects the fact that many crisis situations can be extraordinarily com-plex to manage; emergencies in this category typically include an ele-ment of conflict and disruption of national systems. These problems show that it remains extremely difficult to entirely disentangle politi-cal considerations from decisions over when, and how, to respond to emergency and humanitarian crises. Despite claims the international community's interventions are driven solely on the basis of need,[19] stark differences between the amount, and the types, of humanitarian assistance provided to different countries and in different situations, imply that they are influenced by many complex political, security, commercial, cultural and historical considerations. A larger role for multilateral organisations and NGOs – rather than bilateral agencies – may help mitigate, but not entirely resolve, some of these difficulties. In terms of responding to crises, there is a clear need for a standing **GPI** facility to respond to shocks, national or international.

A case in point: The Global Fund

The rise of the great global funds is generally judged to have been a great success, and non-official givers (such as major foundations) have joined the "traditional" donors in focusing their energies on health and increasing the amount of money available to poor countries to spend on it. The Global Fund to Fight AIDS, Tuberculosis and Malaria is the most successful and innovative mechanism in global health financing. It is also a donor darling – meaning that it regularly receives large disbursements from the official development agencies. Its budget is around US$4 billion a year. Over 90% of funding comes from the ODA budgets of government agencies. The lion's share of the funding for fighting these three diseases comes from the countries themselves, but the Fund is a catalyst, levering domestic investments and incentivising the more difficult but essential investments in commodities as well as sexual and reproductive health and rights (SRHR), human rights and community service delivery.

The Fund is often seen as a UN entity but is actually a Swiss foundation, and a multi-stakeholder partnership that includes the private sector, philanthropic foundations and civil society. Its governance model is therefore unique: contributors have ten board seats and implementers (including civil society and affected communities) have the other ten. Decisions are made on a consensus basis and when voting is required, a two-thirds majority in both blocks (contributors and implementers) is needed. A vibrant advocacy group (Global Fund Advocacy Network) supports and critiques the Global Fund as appropriate, and is instrumental in replenishment processes, which take place every 3 years. More importantly, these advocates work in their countries with their governments on an ongoing basis.

But despite the success of the Global Fund – in terms of money being raised and lives being saved – and despite the way it models many of the principles outlined in this book, it continues to be chronically underfunded; the 3-yearly *Investment Case* report is a political consensus paper, not a reflection of actual funding needs, which are far higher. Traditional donors say they love the Global Fund, but there is never enough money. So what would happen if the **Global Public Investment** approach were introduced to the Global Fund? One could envisage three major shifts.

From voluntary/volatile to orderly/obligatory

Currently donor contributions to the Global Fund are voluntary and therefore volatile, subject to rapidly changing donor priorities (like all ODA). If the economy is slowing (as is currently happening) or if the Global Fund is not delivering against a donor's particular political preference, contribution sizes will be adjusted. Since ODA comes burdened with national priorities, these inevitably feature in discussions of the Global Fund's priorities. The **Global Public Investment** concept assumes a different, more orderly and obligatory funding commitment from all countries, which would mean more – and more predictable – funding. Smaller and poorer countries have continued to increase their contributions; in the replenishment discussions in Lyon in 2019 the Madagascar representative called home and was able to make a pledge of US$1 million.[20] In total 58 countries pledged.

From donor-domination to equal partnership

The current replenishment process is a "donor party" that takes place every three years. It has been very successful, but it has skewed the focus towards bringing the money in, rather than spending it in close collaboration with the major recipients. It is hosted by one (preferably large) donor, and there is little input from the countries that will be implementing most of the work i.e. the net recipients. A **Global Public Investment** approach would change this. All countries would come to the same table and focus not only on contribution levels (these could actually already have been technically prepared elsewhere) but on health objectives and progress. The process would not be about celebrating donors, but all governments that make progress towards collective and jointly agreed goals (aligned with the SDGs).

From exit strategy to prolonged engagement

The Global Fund's policies and practices focus strongly on poverty. Its policy is to withdraw from MICs, guided by GDP data. But most poor people with the highest disease burden live in MICs, where high levels of socio-economic inequality are associated with less favourable health outcomes and vulnerable groups (women and girls, migrants,

sexual minorities) have less access to health services and face higher
levels of stigma and discrimination. This is true in all countries, whatever the income level. That's why advocates are increasingly looking
at health challenges through the lens of *inequality* - it provides a more
logical understanding of where the real needs are, and which investments should take place. Withdrawal of Global Fund support results
in de-funding of prevention, civil society engagement and protection
of vulnerable populations. Under a **Global Public Investment**, GDP
would not be such a defining parameter and "graduation" would be
a thing of the past, so the Global Fund would no longer need to withdraw from middle-income countries.

Gradual progress

We know that concessional development funding is important and
that it needs to undergo various evolutions. But we also know that
the perennial problems with international public money are not going
to disappear any time soon. Mercantilism. Self-interest. Nationalism.
Therefore, we need to work hard to promote best practice and mitigate
poor practice. Just as European regional collaboration started as a
vision and gradually built the appropriate governance arrangement,
the same will happen at a global level. Once we get the theory right, we
have more chance of raising the funds and evolving our international
institutions to spend money as well as possible. No more OECD dominance. An end to unfair shareholdings at the World Bank. More multilateral funds including the full range of governments and stakeholders
to respond to the problems our world faces.

So far it has proved difficult to persuade countries to allocate nationally collected tax revenues to cross-border purposes, and the question
of how to raise sufficient financing for global public goods (GPGs) cannot be separated from *how* these resources should be spent and who
takes key decisions. Should supranational entities intervene to assist in
the supply of GPGs, for example, or should this largely be the preserve
of national entities? As with all spending, public or private, we need
clear outcomes if we want secure inputs. Many institutions, instruments
and funds already exist to channel the kind of money we need, from
the usual bilateral agencies (like NORAD, USAID, the Chinese and
Indian aid ministries) to multilateral stalwarts, like the World Bank and
UN funds. Examples of pooled funding mechanisms to support health
crises include GAVI and UNITAID. If funds like these and the Global
Fund can alter their mandates quickly, to respond to broader objectives
and accommodate a broader governance structure, then they can lead

the effort. If not, we might need a major new fund that embodies modern principles of global cooperation.

While **GPI** is not a form of "global tax" (it is a global fiscal scheme to be financed primarily by *national* taxation) it could be topped up via tax revenue on global transfers (such as a Tobin tax) or international travel (such as an airline levy). While **GPI** is not "global social welfare" – because welfare is best managed at the national level – it does certainly increase global welfare by increasing the supply of global public goods and services both where these are needed locally (within particular nation states) and globally (where nations need to cooperate to supply them). Crucially, we must maintain that the burden of financial responsibility rests with those countries in the Global North with the highest standards of living. In the climate change process, the term "common but differentiated responsibilities" has emerged as a way of emphasising that while all countries have a stake and need to play their part, wealthier countries have a larger pot from which to find the kind of money required to change our world for the better.

Notes

1. How do we fund the refugee crisis? With a Tobin tax: http://www.the-guardian.com/commentisfree/2015/sep/09/fund-refugee-crisis-tobin-tax-world-currency-trading.
2. Killick, Tony, "Politics, evidence and the new aid agenda", published in the *Development Policy Review*, January 2004.
3. Eurodad, Conditionally yours: An analysis of the policy conditions attached to IMF loans, 2014: http://www.eurodad.org/conditionallyyours.
4. Personal communication from World Bank staff.
5. Alesina Alberto and Dollar David, Who Gives Foreign Aid to Whom and Why? (2000) http://www.nber.org/papers/w6612.pdf.
6. United Nations MDG Gap Task Force Report 2015: Taking Stock of the Global Partnership for Development: http://www.un.org/en/development/desa/policy/mdg_gap/mdg_gap2015/2015GAP_FULLREPORT_EN.pdf.
7. Anke Hoeffler and Verity Outram (2008), Need, merit or self-interest – what determines the allocation of aid? http://www.csae.ox.ac.uk/workingpapers/pdfs/2008-19text.pdf.
8. For further information on the OECD-led initiative on aid effectiveness, see: http://www.oecd.org/dac/effectiveness/parisdeclarationandaccraagendaforaction.htm.
9. OECD and UNDP, Making Development Cooperation More Effective, 2019 Progress Report: https://www.oecd.org/dac/making-development-co-operation-more-effective-26f2638f-en.htm
10. The Paris Agenda eventually spawned the Global Partnership for Effective Development Cooperation (GPEDC), established in 2011. These efforts have been complemented by the UN's Development Cooperation

Forum (DCF) which serves as a space to review trends in international development cooperation, and the International Aid Transparency Initiative (IATI) which makes more information available so that spending can be better scrutinized. For further information on the UN's Development Cooperation Forum (DCF), see: http://www.un.org/en/ecosoc/newfunct/develop.shtml. For further information on the International Aid Transparency Initiative (IATI), see: http://www.aidtransparency.net/.

11. https://data.oecd.org/oda/net-oda.htm

12. For more information on the OECD "ODA modernisation" process, see: http://www.oecd.org/dac/financing-sustainable-development/understanding-development-finance.htm.

13. One part of the OECD, the OECD Development Centre, has demonstrated that change is possible, pursuing a far more inclusive approach in recent years. https://www.oecd.org/dev/

14. Adapted and updated from Francisco Sagasti, Keith Bezanson and Fernando Prada, *The Future of Development Financing: Challenges and Strategic Choices*, New York, Palgrave Macmillan, 2005.

15. See NATO: http://www.nato.int/cps/en/natolive/topics_67655.htm.

16. OECD, Multilateral Aid 2015, Better Partnerships for a Post-2015 World: http://www.oecd.org/dac/multilateral-aid-2015-9789264235212-en.htm.

17. BRICS nations to create US$100 billion development bank, 2014: http://www.bbc.com/news/business-28317555.

18. For example, between 1990 and 2011, the combined loan commitments of the Latin American and Caribbean Development Banks, the African Development Bank and the Asian Development Bank increased from US$3 billion to US$28 billion.

19. Humanitarian assistance is supposed to be governed by the principles of humanity, neutrality, impartiality and independence. For further elaboration, see: http://www.globalhumanitarianassistance.org/data-guides/defining-humanitarian-aid.

20. Personal communication from a delegate present.

7 NARRATIVE

From charity to investment

> • *Traditional analysis*: **Foreign aid** is presented as a charitable gift to foreign countries, and as a financial loss in accounting terms.
>
> • *New paradigm*: **Global Public Investment** should be an obligation, the price of living in a decent world, with returns for contributors as well as recipients.

So far we have suggested major changes to the way we understand and manage aid and aid-like finance. But what about the language we use to describe this new approach? What about the story we tell ourselves and the people we hope will support what we are proposing? The NARRATIVE. Often terminology is relegated to an afterthought, a question of communications. But words matter. The way we describe people and things can have practical consequences in the real world. As Southern countries discover a bolder voice on the global stage, criticisms of the traditional language associated with the aid mentality that have been milling for many decades are rising to the fore. Countries are demanding more respectful relationships and less patronising language to accompany the shifting sands of global power.

Unconvincing and old-fashioned

In 2012 a group of researchers asked beneficiaries of aid projects about their experiences and feelings.[1] Although the interviews were carried out in very different parts of the world, the feedback collected was remarkably similar: in short, we appreciate what you are trying to do, and welcome positive impacts in our lives, but we feel disrespected and patronised by the way you work. This is an example from a project in Bosnia-Herzegovina: "We heard from people who felt that they were treated without much respect or consideration. Such treatment was an insult to their dignity... A few people said that international agencies claim to be 'partners' with their beneficiaries or local organizations, but then behave as the owners/bosses. One local NGO representative talked about walking out of a presentation by an international organization – she found it so arrogantly and condescendingly presented that she could not bear to stay". People that "give aid", from government officials to civil society to philanthropists, are considered arrogant and distant, despite meaning well. Bureaucratic incentives and the attempt in recent years to become more "business-like" by copying private sector approaches contribute to the feeling that while specific outputs are much welcomed, people view the cumulative impacts of aid quite negatively.

This patronising attitude is not just the preserve of foreigners, by any means. Indrajit Roy, an academic, has written the story of a community of landless labourers in Bihar, the poorest region of India.[2] Their habitations were congested and they lacked water and sanitation, but they resisted all attempts to relocate them. Why? Not because they didn't realise the need for change – they did want better houses, but not at any price. The labourers belonged to the Dalit caste and were considered "untouchable" by the elite classes; they were not being treated with respect, involved in decision-making, participating as equals. Change, said one of Roy's interviewees, is when we can look our landlords in the eyes as equals, not as inferiors. Roy called his article "Development as Dignity". The labourers wanted "development" but not at the cost of their equality and self-worth – the right to decide on their own futures and priorities.

The decision of the landless Bihar community makes little sense in traditional economic terms, according to which we are effectively walking wallets, always looking for material improvements in well-being. But increasingly communities, social movements and politicians recognise that while most of us do, of course, pursue material security, few people operate *solely* at that level. One thing is more important than money and material well-being. Dignity. That's why people leave their jobs where they are being mistreated, despite the hit to their earnings. That's why people take a stand against racism and injustice, aware of the potential consequences for themselves. That's why the woman walked out of the aid presentation in Bosnia-Herzegovina. The thinking that underpins much development cooperation has to change if we are to make the case for **Global Public Investment** in a new era. We need a new narrative. We need to communicate this new reality and vision to publics in both Global North (where support is waning) and Global South (where there is cynicism about old types of "aid"). Crucially, the new narrative will enable the more profound changes we need in policy and international relations as well.

From development to sustainability

For too long a binary has been propagated between countries that call themselves "developed" and those that are supposedly "developing". The MDGs, for example, were intended for "developing" countries, while "developed" countries had no goals or targets for themselves, just contributions to help other parts of the world. This attitude, whose roots are firmly planted in the colonial era, may finally be on its last legs. Foreign aid was conceived as something done by "rich" countries in support of "poor" countries when the world was more easily characterised by a "rich-poor", divide. The universality of the SDGs, breaking that patronising separation between developed and developing countries, implies a new era of equal treatment, whereby standards of living enjoyed by the wealthiest countries should now be in the purview of historically poorer ones. The SDGs are *universal*; no longer can we talk about one set of countries that needs to be economically "developed" vis-à-vis another "already developed" set.

For readers of this book that don't live in "developing" countries, try this thought experiment. How would you feel if the part of the country you are from, your county or region or city, were described as "developing" and contrasted with other parts of your country that were defined as "developed". Wouldn't it be demeaning? Wouldn't it have a material impact on how you and community felt about yourselves, your confidence, your pride. In most countries it would simply not be considered politically correct at all. And yet this language continues to be in constant use in the world of international development.

An important implication of a focus on sustainability is that, unlike poverty, which is located (mainly) in poor countries, the problem now being discussed is located in all countries: unsustainable development. Addressing it requires profound structural transformations across countries of *all* income levels (with differentiated levels of responsibilities). The problem to which sustainable development is the answer is certainly poverty, but it is also affluence and excessive consumption, the consequences of capitalism gone rampant, with insufficient oversight and management. In contrast to previous eras of development, when lines were starkly drawn between "developed" and "developing", and the challenges we faced were contained largely within the boundaries of nation-states, the common challenges we now face, along with shifting geopolitical patterns, mean that, today, all countries are developing. Many countries are wary of losing this division, because they worry that wealthier countries will try to wheedle their way out of their global obligations. But it is not hard to divide countries into categories without using patronising and misleading language. The climate finance talks simply use the neutral term Annexes within which different countries are categorised, for example.

The *sustainable development* paradigm even calls into question the idea of convergence which has inspired development thinking and practice for the last five decades. Rather than all countries following the path of the industrialised – known by some as "getting to Denmark", considered the world's most developed country – what is now needed is for *all* countries to take a different path towards progress that is compatible with the earth's environmental limits.

From charity to mutual benefit

The charity paradigm has long been considered patronising by poorer countries and is increasingly considered old-fashioned even in many "donor" agencies. The reality that strategic and economic interests have always been at play in "aid-giving" is recognised by most traditional donors somewhat cautiously, but is openly acknowledged by the "emerging" contributors of development cooperation in the Global South who eschew the term aid because of its simplistic connotations, preferring the language of mutual benefit. They want to imply horizontal relationships between equals, similar to business transactions between partners. There is a place for charity, of course, but while charity is bestowed by the haves on the have-nots, **Global Public Investment** is committed by all for the good of all. The language of "aid" and "donors" needs to become a thing of the past. It doesn't recognise the benefits to the donor that almost always accompany an aid relationship, either directly in a specific exchange, or indirectly through some kind of longer-term economic or political benefit. **Global Public Investment** is not charity, but a demonstration of responsibility for global welfare.

There are plenty of elements of the aid narrative that we need to hold on to (including the encouraging notion of generosity to the less fortunate) but there are aspects that need to evolve. Indeed, the very word "aid" is one of the things we need to ditch, as many have already observed.[3] In 2011, the Busan Declaration relegated the word "aid" to only occasional use, while the then Chair of the OECD DAC explicitly suggesting ditching the word. The concept of mutual benefit is already firmly embedded in South-South Cooperation rhetoric, and needs to become more common among traditional "aid" agencies.

As Simon Reid-Henry has persuasively written: "While some see **GPI** as an opportunity to repurpose a dysfunctional aid system (and it is certainly that), one of its greatest values is that it offers a way of extending the *political obligations* that derive from domestic and (for Europeans) regional level fiscal relationships to the international scale. Aid can never do that because it is always unidirectional and creates uneven power relationships. Systems where everybody contributes, however, have a different effect. We don't create 'moral' relationships with our fellow national citizens when we pay our taxes, for example, and mostly we aren't asked to think 'morally' about where our tax monies are going. Instead we agree simply to all fund the basic things a functioning society needs – from roads through to free education – and in doing so, over time, we create a web of political obligations. We don't then micromanage what is done with our tax dollars. But we do hold politicians accountable for the way they spend it (e.g. what they prioritise, whether they spend it wisely). The same holds at the international level. We do not need 'global democracy' to establish a very basic web of fiscal interdependencies and a great deal then begins to take care of itself. That is what **Global Public Investment** ultimately is: an investment in realising a greater social future".

Global Public Investment need not always be spent abroad; it can sometimes be spent in the contributor country in pursuit of international objectives. Especially in the areas of research and science, considerable resources may be spent within national borders even though most of the intended beneficiaries are located in other countries. For example, the public sector supplies about 51% of current investments in malaria research and development, some of which is spent in high-income contributor nations on basic research and product development.[4] Price reductions in technology have been responsible for some of the most important progress in development,[5] and investing much more money into researching key public interest issues (such as diseases and clean technology) is likely to result in cheaper, better technology, appropriate to specific contexts. Other "non-flow" examples of **Global Public Investment** are support for immigrants and education about international human rights and sustainable development.

From cost to investment[6]

Aid has traditionally been seen as a cost to the taxpayer, a payment used for consumption with no return for the contributing country. We should view the money the world spends on itself not as gift but as investment, not only on the sustainable infrastructure and institutions our world needs, but also in the social sectors. Money spent on health and education is an investment with returns for human progress, just as spending money on educational or healthy activities for our children is an investment in our family. This reframing could make resource transfers more accountable, shifting from charitable donations to contracts with accountability, transparency, recognition of possible failure and evaluation as key elements of a longer-term relationship. The word "investment" conveys a much stronger sense that there is a return for the investor and reflects the way health, education and other public investments are described domestically. Some organisations working on global development, including the Global Fund, already use the concept of "investment" widely.[7]

The copious academic literature on foreign private investment in the Global South (particularly foreign direct investment) is instructive for many aspects of this debate. It is contested, but there is clear agreement on one thing: FDI only works for the host country under certain conditions. The three factors that seem to make FDI more or less supportive of development objectives (as opposed simply to the profit of the investor) are: country context (the "prior" conditions), type of FDI (the nature of the investment and decisions made by investors) and the policies governing FDI (decisions made by host governments to actively manage FDI). These factors could equally well apply to international public spending and could encourage a more profound understanding of "effectiveness". This literature should inform debates about **Global Public Investment** rather than being siloed off as a separate research topic. Furthermore, separating foreign spending into public and private is complicated by the active role played by the state in economic and business affairs in many countries. Whereas the stark separation of the two realms has been common, at least in rhetoric, in traditional "donor" economies, it is much more fluid in many of the emerging economies, including the BRICS. Both public and private investment can support growth and development, but when and where is a matter of context and political decisions.

The investment analogy has its limits, naturally. Most private investment is made for profit, while interventions in the field of international cooperation seek primarily to further internationally agreed development objectives. Therefore, using the language of foreign investment should not be seen as denying the element of solidarity inherent in development cooperation. Instead, it could add a further layer to our conceptualisation of aid, and encourage us to move beyond the "recipient of charity" mentality, towards mutuality and working together for agreed outcomes.

From foreign to global

For all this talk of global public health and global public goods, is anyone talking about the "global public"? We don't seem to even have that phrase in our lexicon. Looking at Europe, it is possible that five decades of union have led to a meaningful European public. Has this contributed to support for the redistribution of funds between EU countries? Undoubtedly. While the mechanism is far from perfect, and while many criticise it (particularly recently, and particularly in my country, the UK), a system of large-scale redistribution has taken place continent-wide to support regionally agreed priorities, such as environmental sustainability, green infrastructure and transport, social welfare and business support.

Such a consciousness also exists in Africa, where pan-Africanism has had its peaks and troughs but underpins the African Union and its many joint funds (including the African Centres for Disease Control and Prevention that has come to the fore in the Covid-19 crisis). In Latin America, where I live, the shared heritage has not yet resulted in significant solidarity spending although the regional banks are active. And Asia's size and political divisions may be holding back a similar union in that continent, although, again, sub-regional bodies like the Association of Southeast Asian Nations (ASEAN) and the South Asian Association for Regional Cooperation (SAARC) have been enhanced by this Covid-19 crisis. The more these regions think as regions, with a regional public not just lots of national publics, the more likely they will be able to pool resources to combat regional problems and promote regional sustainability and, yes, convergence and equality – as Europe has shown.

So can we hope for the same at the global level. In a sense, it is what many civil society organisations and visionary politicians have been working towards for decades. The United Nations itself is some kind of proto-attempt at building global concern and commitment. But we have not, as far as I know, termed it in the same terms as we do at the national level, where we talk about "the general public", "public-spirited", "public spending", "the public interest". This language implies togetherness, a commitment to the whole, a society. At the global level we prefer the language of aid to others, solidarity with others, sympathy for others. It is still "us and them", rather than just "us".

It is not that you need a fully functioning global public before you can start on global public goods, including health. But the success and effectiveness of global public good provision will be proportionate to the strength of global public consciousness. So while we need solid emergency leadership in the short term to respond to this crisis moment, we need visionary thinking as well, to build a new idea, the idea of a global public, which should be attended to in just the same way our national and regional publics are. Especially as recession bites in many Western countries, some feel that limited resources should be focused on their own people rather than spent on foreign aid. There are responses that can be made to this logic, not least that the standard of living in aid donor countries remains far ahead of aid recipient countries, even if the donors are currently in recession and the recipients growing fairly well. In other words, there is a long way to go before wealthier countries can declare their moral obligations at an end.

We should consider **Global Public Investment** as support not just to other countries but to the global commons. It has long been recognised that poverty and conflict anywhere in the world can be a threat to stability and prosperity in places thousands of miles away. In the era of climate change and planetary resource limits this is ever truer. Expanding our horizons to include foreign countries as part of our responsibility is a significant conceptual frontier, but it is logical as global communication improves and our world shrinks. We need a firm shift in rhetoric away from the idea that countries are paying for other people's development, and towards an understanding of our shared destiny. In most countries, wealthier parts pay a premium in taxes to support less well-off regions, or investment in public goods, even if they do not use them. Just as at the national level citizens accept the concept of taxation to pay for national public goods (welfare, conservation, national parks, policing and defence, infrastructure) so we need to develop language to make that analogy at a global level. The institutions and modalities will be very different, but the fundamental concept is the same. In public communications, cooperation is generally seen as country-focused i.e. wealthier countries help poorer ones solve national challenges, and this remains the core of the work. But in the SDG era we should see national challenges (whether in health, education, inequality, etc.) as global challenges affecting everyone in the world.

From temporary to permanent

Although the theories behind aid-giving have varied and evolved, there has been one constant – they have all been based on the idea that aid is temporary, a stop gap while poorer countries "catch up" with richer ones. Most people still assume that sooner or later (and many think sooner) aid agencies will "do themselves out of a job" as countries begin to rely exclusively on domestic revenue and private international flows. But there is one major difference between the struggle to end "absolute poverty" on the one hand, and the fight for equality and sustainability on the other. While it is conceivable, and on balance even probable, that the world will all but eradicate extreme poverty within a period of decades, the challenge of inequality and unsustainability will be perennial. It is possible to reduce levels of inequality both at an international level (between countries) and nationally (between citizens of the same country), as has been proven in some regions of the world in the past 50 years. But any sensible analysis of human history or present-day political conditions will conclude that, while it has peaks and troughs, inequality has been a constant aspect of human societies. And there is no reason to conclude that the investments required to green our economies are going to reduce in urgency in the foreseeable future. International cooperation is not going anywhere.

This is also true of the challenge of sustainability – whether at the national, regional or global level there will always be new challenges for the public realm to respond to, and that will require money. Our broadening appreciation of the sustainable development challenges the world faces implies the clear need for resource transfers to continue *over the long term* to drive forward a sustainable model of development, even in a world in which extreme poverty is eradicated. There is no future scenario in which such funds will not play an important role, despite their proportionately smaller quantity compared to other sources. Rather than coming slowly to an end as the world succeeds in tackling poverty, the international development project may only just be beginning.

Climate finance is a great example of the contradiction at the heart of the aid mentality. On the one hand, "aid" is being reduced to middle-income countries such as India, according to the conventional theory of aid. But on the other, public climate finance is meant to be increased to those very same countries. But public climate finance is no different in substance to aid – in fact, OECD countries include international public climate finance in their aid budgets. It is the same money. The only difference is the rhetoric. And rhetoric matters. Aid is associated with charity, with the donor/recipient relationship. Countries like India reject this as patronising. But climate finance is offered as the price paid for an historic wrong, the pollution which is largely the responsibility of the most industrialised countries. Countries like

India accept this as logical and appropriate. Furthermore, climate finance is an outrider for two important new principles we need to see emerge – that **Global Public Investment** should be contributory, not voluntary, and that decisions need to be made at the UN rather than in smaller clubs of countries, such as the OECD.

While it will certainly remain true that all countries will be keen to end aid *dependency* (whereby aid flows make up a substantial part of national spending for a prolonged period of time), our new vision for **Global Public Investment** would see it as a permanent fixture on the development landscape, always at hand to support sustainable development, global goods, poverty initiatives and humanitarian emergencies. The ability of countries to access private funds is welcome, and the necessity to increase domestic resources is clear. But there is no reason to believe that the usefulness of **GPI** will somehow decrease. On the contrary, its possibilities only increase as potential recipients become more empowered and assertive, meaning that the well-known downsides of aid dependency become less problematic. The aid industry needs to alter its narrative, explaining to the public and politicians that our financial contributions to global development are not temporary – as had previously been implied – but permanent. That might help end the constant media debate about whether to give aid and how much it should be. It must be a permanent feature of the modern global economy.

Notes

1. https://usaidlearninglab.org/events/time-listen-hearing-people-receiving-end-international-aid.
2. https://www.tandfonline.com/doi/abs/10.1080/13600818.2013.835392.
3. See my article in the Guardian almost 10 years ago: https://www.theguardian.com/global-development/poverty-matters/2011/jul/27/aid-and-development-coordination.
4. Policy Cures, From Pipeline to Product: Malaria R&D funding needs into the next decade, 2013: http://www.malariavaccine.org/files/RD-report-December2013.pdf.
5. See Charles Kenny, (2011) Getting Better: Why Global Development Is Succeeding--And How We Can Improve the World Even More
6. This section builds on an article I wrote with Andy Sumner: https://www.theguardian.com/global-development/2015/aug/05/aid-should-be-seen-as-foreign-public-investment-not-just-charity.
7. The UN Millennium Project's 2005 report on financing the MDGs was called "Investing in Development" – one of many examples: https://www.who.int/hdp/publications/4b.pdf.

8   Towards internationalism

"Most of the things worth doing in the world have been declared impossible before they were done".

Louis D. Brandeis

Structural problems require structural responses

While this book argues that **Global Public Investment** will be a crucial part of any attempt to respond to global challenges in the decades to come, it would be wrong to think it is the only or even the most important change needed to ensure global harmony and sustainability. Perhaps the biggest criticism of aid is the way it has usurped policies that might matter a great deal more to a country's development. Aid always gets top bill somehow, despite the fact that by any sensible measure it is only the top priority in a handful of very poor or small countries. This book has focused on revisiting our understanding of international public finance in a new era, but we should not exaggerate its importance relative to other major global policy issues. Delivering our global goals will require collective international action on an immense scale, and that will include the mobilisation of unprecedented levels of cooperation. Finance is only a part of what is needed.

To achieve the SDGs and a healthier planet, if every sense, we need to do much more than spend money. For example, for progress on hunger the world needs to increase investment in rural infrastructure, improve plant and livestock gene banks, eliminate agricultural export subsidies and limit food price volatility by sharing market information better. Many reforms, both national and international, are required to create an "enabling environment" to achieve progress: creating a fairer trading system and more stable global financial system to encourage developmentally useful private foreign investments, reducing illicit capital flows and tax evasion and increasing stolen-asset recovery; international agreements on money laundering, illicit trade and arms trading that reflect the true global costs of such activities for global peace and security. The Tax Justice Network estimates that the global loss to governments from profit shifting by multinational companies, for instance, is upwards of US$500 billion per year. They further estimate that governments are losing at least US$189 billion a year as a result of tax dodging. The countries of the Global South are the hardest hit.[1]

Structural transformation is required in wealthier countries, whose growth pattern has set the world on a path to unsustainability, just as much as poorer ones. Most countries are still pursuing traditional forms of economic development through carbon-intensive forms of industrialisation and the international community is still thinking through how to manage growing global risks, vulnerabilities and uncertainties on a long-term basis. Structural transformation in poorer countries – moving beyond agriculture and resource extraction towards manufacturing and technological innovation – will be required for countries to maintain spending on infrastructure, social investments and other public goods, as well as climate mitigation, adaptation and restoration. SDG17 is a consolidated list of actions which countries and other bodies need to take to reach the 16 preceding goals. It envisages a "global partnership" in which everyone is supposed to work in concertto achieve progress on everything from finance and trade to technology transfer and capacity building.

So it has been an important step forward, even if an obvious one, that the non-aid elements of the enabling environment are now commonly recognised as central to achieving the SDGs – this has been a central achievement of the "beyond aid" movement. But the finance is crucial as well. It is also the main ground of debate in the development sector, for good or ill. While more and more attention is rightly being paid to broader questions of how countries can cooperate for global and national development, 60 years of building up an aid edifice mean that questions as to its future are pertinent. Furthermore, while many in the development industry may be moving on from an over-tight focus on aid, the general public still tends to consider aid the primary means by which wealthier peoples can help poorer ones. It is possible that reframing the debate – understanding that these issues are global concerns that matter to everyone, rather than foreign concerns that matter to people far away – could also help move the debate on in other crucial areas of national and international policymaking, such as trade rules, climate policy and illicit financial flows.

Two main barriers

One of the most common responses to this proposal is that, while it is certainly needed, **Global Public Investment** is politically unfeasible, as countries seem to be retreating into nationalism. When I first proposed a prototype version of **Global Public Investment** in 2012, the idea was met with baffled silence and possibly some muffled laughter at the back of the conference room. "Unrealistic" was the most generous comment it received that day. Since then gradually it has become a less radical idea until, today, especially as Covid-19 reorganises our political priorities both at home and abroad, more and more people are beginning to see its possibilities. In this final chapter we will look at the political and other barriers preventing us shifting to a system of **GPI**, and why those barriers might be diminishing one by one.

Much of the traditional aid sector appears still to be in denial about the shift in ambition from the MDG to the SDG era and has spent the last 5 years, since the SDGs were signed in 2015, carefully paying them no more than lip-service. This attitude was clear even during the long period of negotiation that led to the signing of the Sustainable Development Goals when there were essentially two negotiating camps: those who preferred a kind of MDG-plus set of goals, still closely focused on extreme poverty objectives (mainly the "donor" countries in the Global North and their campaign partners); and those who were arguing for something more expansive, a holistic vision for a fairer world (generally including Southern governments). There is no doubt which side won. The traditional donors lost, in part, because their more limited vision was no longer compatible with the new context of international relations in which Southern countries voice their opinions and perspectives much more powerfully. But although the more expansive vision won on paper, the people with the purse strings have been slow to change. If a shift to **Global Public Investment** is so obviously needed to respond to all the world's challenges, why is it so hard to get it going? Why such a lethargic response to 21st century realities? There are two main reasons – theoretical and political – and they reinforce each other.

First, there is still no good understanding of the role of concessional public money for international priorities. We are stuck in a 20th-century understanding of aid, and there is no alternative theory doing the rounds – until now. Even in universities, students of development studies are increasingly not studying aid, but other topics. This is a mistake. International public finance remains a critical part of the overall development ecosystem – it can be used powerfully for good and bad – and we need to analyse it to understand it better. If we are to halt this trend and build up a new pot of international public finance to deliver the SDGs, then we are going to need a much more powerful theory of why it is needed and how it can be spent effectively. The landscape of contributions has changed dramatically but the traditional conceptualisation of "aid" does not allow for this evolution. We need to get our analysis straight, and avoid logical fallacies. Prioritising scarce resources should not be confused with assessing actual need. It is true that much of the West remains in conditions of austerity following a very serious financial meltdown 10 years ago, and now with Covid-19 to boot, and it is therefore understandable that all budgets are under great pressure, including the aid budget. But that does not mean there is less need – it means it is harder to muster the political will to provide for that need. The **Global Public Investment** proposal still needs more work, but it is the basis of a bold new way to understand international public spending for sustainable development.

The second major reason for slow progress on **Global Public Investment** is political. Wealthier countries might not be getting away with their lack of generosity quite so easily if strong intellectual arguments were being made to resist their political choices. But the political barriers to supporting **Global Public Investment** remain substantial, even with a convincing new theory. The current political and economic context in wealthy countries means it is hard to get sustainable support for international contributions. The main reason purse strings are being tied up again is that the traditional donors see an opportunity to decrease their contributions to poverty reduction and global public goods. It suits them to have an excuse, so they argue that the money is "no longer needed".

As the Global South rises, so the traditionally powerful Global North is facing economic and political challenges it has not seen for almost a century. The financial crash of the late 2000s ended a long period of growth and austere economic circumstances have led to a resurgence of populism and nationalism in many western countries, with a consequent undermining of internationalist rhetoric that dominated for some years. And now Covid-19 has hit. This political reality is somewhat in tension with the bold global ambitions signed up to by world leaders in September 2015 and it means the rapid increases in ODA that accompanied the first decade of this century and the MDG era have not been matched at the onset of the SDG era.

If the barriers are theoretical and political, then our response needs to be both intellectual and organisational. First, the realisation that large amounts of public money will be required at a global level for the foreseeable future, and quite probably in perpetuity, to help achieve the public goods that we all want to see, from environmental protection, to peace and security, to poverty reduction. Based on this realisation, the second step is to work out how to galvanise that money, and manage it effectively for the good of all. This involves transforming a system intended as a stop gap while countries caught up to so-called developed status into a permanent fixture on the international landscape. The governance problems will be obvious – but the other option, to let private money rule the international roost, and depend on individual states, or groups of them, to pursue publicly agreed objectives is significantly worse. And it is important to get the theory right to support the political campaigning. If countries can't or won't pay for global needs, fine, but they shouldn't hide behind the excuse that their support isn't needed by using an outdated theory.

Building public support

Overall, states still find it very difficult to allocate nationally collected tax revenues to cross-border purposes (unless there is a clear and visible domestic advantage). And as with all public expenditures, states will carefully evaluate whether international spending is in their strategic interest versus other ways they could spend these resources. The challenge is that citizens – and their elected representatives – often don't prioritise this spending. They may not know, care or fully appreciate how this spending directly affects them and their families. Voters may respond to a major event or catastrophe, but will typically underestimate the benefits of expenditures on international programmes. Increased competition in the international financing "marketplace" as well as, more recently, austerity programmes in many traditional donor economies have helped to drive the so-called "results" agenda where resources are allocated to initiatives that promise high social and environmental returns with as little risk or burden to national budgets as possible (more "bang for the buck"). The risks associated with this strategy, of course, are that some higher-risk countries (e.g. fragile states) and higher-risk thematic areas (e.g. governance and infrastructure investments) become even more underfunded.

There has been a trend over recent years for large donor countries to emphasise the *domestic* benefits of their aid programmes. Several, including Australia, Canada and the UK, have even brought their international development agencies under the umbrella of foreign affairs and trade ministries. Former Australian Prime Minister Tony Abbot said of his decision to effectively abolish Australia Aid in 2013,

"We're going to bring aid back inside the [foreign affairs] department because we want Australia's aid program to be fully integrated into our overall diplomatic effort. We don't want our diplomacy going in one direction and our aid program going in another direction".[2] The same argument was made by the British government when it abolished DFID in 2020. But while it is generally accepted that emerging economies may describe their financial assistance in terms of mutual benefit, traditional donors are often lambasted for similar messages. Oxfam rebuked UK Chancellor, George Osborne, recently when he said: "The question is not just how does our aid budget help the rest of the world, but how does it help Britain's national interest?" The NGO pointed to the high proportion of British companies, researchers, consultancies and technical advisers benefiting from the UK's aid programme.[3] This is a topic of continued discussion. Often, the "domestic benefit" angle provides an easier sell to a sometimes sceptical electorate. But the fundamental importance of redistribution and reparation from Global North to South cannot be lost.

The US is relatively upfront about the mixed motivations for its financial assistance. USAID describes its mission, vision and values as: "[To] partner [with developing countries] to end extreme poverty and to promote resilient, democratic societies while advancing our security and prosperity".[4] Many emerging contributors of the Global South emphasise that South-South Cooperation is defined by reciprocity and mutual benefit.[5] India, for example, states that its engagement promotes "a mutually beneficial exchange of development experiences and resources".[6] Benefits to the provider might not come directly – helping countries reduce their climate emissions, for example, is a classic example of contributing to the global common good with benefits to all somewhere down the line. Helping another country develop industry may lead to better trading relationships with the provider country (and also with many other countries) but, again, that might take many years to manifest. These divisions are by no means mutually exclusive. Economic development may be a significant motivation for development assistance because it alleviates human suffering. But it can also provide other benefits for contributors because it promotes trade and investment, and may enhance security. One of the radical aspects of the **Global Public Investment** approach is that even rich countries could benefit directly from investments in poorer communities or interventions to support global public goods, just as richer members of the European Union also receive grants from the EU budget – they are net contributors but do see some money come back their way. This could be an attractive new idea to people in wealthy countries.

One of the great lessons from recent years in European and US politics is that place matters, community matters. Conservative politicians have won support for programmes that prioritise the local and the national while liberals have suffered from an association with globalisation. This is a serious challenge for those of us that believe in internationalism, that the life of people everywhere should be valued the same. But it is also a profound truth that often the right has grasped better than the left. It is not narrow or racist, as some have implied, to cherish tradition and community – it is natural and celebratory. Somehow, as we build a politics fit for the 21st century, we must balance the need to build a global public and provide global public goods, with the need to preserve and cherish the local. "Think global, act local" has been one common motto to try to achieve that balance, but we probably need to go further. We need to think and act both local and global if we are to balance local issues that dominate the lives of most of us, with global-mindedness and equality, which are increasingly the *sine qua non* of human survival wherever you live. Action will lead to benefits for all countries, just as inaction will lead to problems for all. There is mixed evidence on public support for international cooperation in traditional donor countries, but some evidence suggests that western publics respond positively to the idea that aid might help prevent a pandemic reaching their shores – so the Covid-19 moment is a critical time to make the case for change.

The coronavirus moment

It may be that it takes a cataclysmic event like Covid-19 to persuade decision makers and the general public that global health is worth the investment. But it clearly has not persuaded everyone! In May 2020 Donald Trump announced a huge cut to the world's leading global health institution, the World Health Organisation. While we can be sure that global spending on health will change as a result of this crisis, how it does so will depend on the influencing power and creativity of civil society and others. So one thing is clear: the campaign for **Global Public Investment** is only just beginning.

It is tempting for countries to retreat into narrow nationalism. This is always a mistake, but especially when faced with a disease that crosses borders with such ease. The western world's working classes, for example, face profound challenges when it comes to jobs and opportunities coming out of the global lockdown initiated in response to this pandemic. It is understandable that community and national leaders, especially those on the left, will need to focus tightly on the needs of more vulnerable domestic constituencies. But there can be no sustainable response to the challenges faced in the West which does not respond as well to the often far greater challenges in poorer countries. Covid-19 represents what economists call a "weakest link" problem: solve it everywhere, in other words, or see it continue to rear its head at home.

For this virus is not done yet.[7] The forced interdependencies of market globalisation cannot be managed except by collective action at the international level. What might be termed "fiscal internationalism" is one part of that collective action: more public money paying for better public goods and basic services, internationally as well as nationally, and more democratic governance of that money, upending a decision-making structure which still reflects the power structures and political thinking of the 1950s more than the 2020s. Today progressives cannot win at home unless they win globally as well. Responding to the present global public health crisis with a form of **Global Public Investment** would be a concrete and important first step to realising that better future for all.

Attempts to overhaul the financial system, instigate better trade rules and debt workout mechanisms, and a host of other systemic issues, are not new. They feature strongly in the 2002 Monterrey Financing for Development consensus – a clear mandate for change. But they have only progressed at a snail's pace. Structural change is inherently difficult to achieve, compared with increasing aid, which while difficult (especially in times of economic austerity) is still relatively easier (as it doesn't require international consensus).

Global Public Investment has the potential to achieve a great many things. But it is at heart a relatively modest change in our existing way of doing things, and it requires a relatively modest re-purposing of our existing national and international institutions to achieve. This has been done before. During the First World War the allied powers were forced to cooperate to ensure the supply of essential goods needed to keep the war effort going, a system that in some respects provided the practical relationships that became the basis of the League of Nations. More widely remembered moments include the creation of the Bretton Woods institutions (such as the World Bank and the IMF) at the end of the Second World War, or the conservative counter-revolution within those same organisations during the international economic crises of the 1970s. The current moment requires making the case for a similar "step change" in the usual order of things again.

There remain a great many important questions of principle and practice alike that need working through to bring something like **Global Public Investment** into existence. But these can be answered in time. The critical question is: can the political moment for something like this be seized as it was by the Keynesians in the 1930s and 1940s and the Neoliberals in the 1970s and 1980s? Those were both transformations in monetary policy above all else. The transformation that is needed now is in the realm of fiscal policy which has lagged resolutely behind these earlier upheavals. Covid-19 opens up the political case for that transformation to now be made. As the 1978 World Development Report argued over 40 years ago, "Additional external resources cannot guarantee either accelerated growth or success in dealing with poverty, but the absence of adequate resources greatly increases the probability of failure".[8]

From nationalism to internationalism

International development has reached a crucial moment in its evolution. The paradigm of North-South development assistance is now outdated. All countries are engaged in contributing to global development, supporting sustainability and poverty reduction locally, nationally, regionally and globally. At the same time, the challenges faced by the world, in particular the poorer countries, are evolving and, to some extent, multiplying. The SDGs firmed up an agenda in which ending absolute poverty remains central but other concerns are also recognised, including the need to reduce growing inequality, and the need to invest in greener growth within the planet's environmental limits. Although I called Chapter 3 "from survive to thrive", the threats to the planet from environmental degradation, and to cohesive societies from increasing inequality, have led other analysts to worry that we are moving back again simply to survival mode – an attitude that seems to be echoed by the climate strikers and other youth movements.

In this context, the future of development aid is the subject of heated debate. Is it still needed? Who should give it? How should it evolve? In my view, the era of international financial cooperation is not ending; it is still in its infancy. This is evidenced by the plethora of new agencies, both public and private, to emerge in recent years to complement, or challenge, traditional sources of funds. But people in many aid-giving countries are not so sure (to say the least). They question the simplistic "aid works" narrative; assertions that aid is responsible for impressive improvements in human development in the past couple of decades are hard to substantiate. More fundamentally, perhaps, they find sending large amounts of money abroad hard to justify when times are hard at home. The thinking that underpins development cooperation has to change if we are to make the case for a new era. We need a new vision, a new approach and a new narrative. That is why, building on the trust of the general public in the national level public sector, I have proposed **five paradigm shifts** for a new international public finance model for global development in the 21st century.

While some of the paradigm shifts set out in this book may seem radical, they are mostly a reflection of the changes already underway in the development cooperation sector. Both South-South Cooperation and, increasingly, "traditional" donors are acting in this new way. But they lack a coherent understanding to explain why. We need to move on from confusion to clarity, because while much of this evolution is taking place organically, there is still much to fight for in terms of quantity, quality and governance. Moving in the direction I propose, we could see a stronger campaign for global development in (at least) the following ways:

- The new approach will mobilise stronger and more sustainable support for *significantly more* concessional international public finance being made available to support global goals and complement other types of finance.
- With more in the pot, the inelegant competition between different sectors and countries could be somewhat diminished. Low-income countries would remain the main concern of the international community, but middle-income countries could continue to benefit from **Global Public Investment** according to assessed need.
- The negative effects of transition and graduation out of aid will cease. Quite the opposite – **Global Public Investment** will be useful in countries at all income levels.
- The new approach could usher in *new governance models* in which the process of development finance will be jointly steered by net-recipient countries based on their own investment plans, specifying when, where and how **Global Public Investment** can contribute.
- The role of major global funding mechanisms (such as, in the health sector, Global Fund, GAVI and UNITAID) could change from channelling donor funding towards facilitation of the eco-system of **Global Public Investment**.
- Current development practice could change for the better, with new players using their influence and instincts to complement more "traditional" contributors. Each country and region would have its own approach, with *mutual learning* across the world.

- For the first time, development (as defined through the 17 SDGs) will be treated as a global common good to which all countries contribute.
- **Global Public Investment** would focus as much on embedding systems, responding to long-term structural threats and spurring research into global solutions as it would on urgent responses to disaster and chronic poverty.

We say we need to pull out all the stops, but we cannot clarify the future of one of the most important pieces of the development puzzle. We say we understand the higher SDG ambitions, but we act as if we are still working under the old paradigm. We say we recognise the different roles of private, philanthropic and public money, but we still engage in "gap" calculations as if all money is interchangeable. We say we want to save the planet, but we continue to offer minor sums of global public money to safeguard global public goods and services. We say we need to move on from aid, but we don't know where to move to.

Embracing a more ambitious and coherent approach will help resolve these contradictions and ensure sustained investment in things that matter to the world. Of course, a more modern understanding of concessional IPF, now rebranded as **Global Public Investment**, will be only a part of the conundrum. And no-one suggests that the changes proposed in this book could happen overnight; ingrained beliefs and incentives will take time to evolve, and words are just words until actions and policy decisions also shift. Rather, they are a direction of travel that the aid and international development sector could take over the coming years.

The current aid system is unfit to respond to the problems facing the world and its individual countries. In this book I have argued that in place of volatile, top-down forms of "aid", we need a system of fixed, universal and multi-directional fiscal allocations capable of meeting the complex collective needs of *all* national societies and the world as a whole. And the three words in **GPI** point to three crucial aspects of this new system. First, it needs to be **global** in the sense that all countries contribute and all receive, rich and poor alike. Second, it needs to be **public** in the sense that it upholds the specific qualities of public money: accountable to all those who pay in, directed at public goods, services and infrastructure, and committed over the longer term. Third, it is **investment**, with a strong focus on grants not loans, intended to realise longer-term social and economic gain, either through building social infrastructure for greater social cohesion, or through securing the provision pathways of complex global public goods, such as climate change mitigation, which would otherwise go under-supplied (if left to individual nations and private actors alone).[9]

While it will seem like a radical new direction for some, I hope I have shown how it is in keeping with the ambitions of the international community and is quite similar to a number of projects already underway in various parts of the world. It won't solve all the world's problems by any means, and it will be beset by many of the problems that have confronted ambitious internationalist projects of the past. But it is the best option for a humanity that wants not only to survive, but to live in peace and prosperity.

The international community needs to break out of its comfort zone. Its responsibility does not come to an end when extreme poverty is eliminated, nor when basic health coverage is achieved for all, nor when countries turn "middle-income". It persists as long as there is inequality of access and services within and between countries, and as long as global public goods need preserving and expanding – a high ideal, but one that is appropriate for our times, and increasingly accepted as the inevitable corollary of the SDG vision. The job of the international development community is not to "do itself out of a job" but to write the next chapter of international cooperation for sustainable development. **Global Public Investment** must play a pivotal role.

Notes

1. https://www.taxjustice.net/topics/more/estimates-of-tax-avoidance-and-evasion/.
2. Troilo, Pete, Inside the takedowns of AusAID and CIDA, 2015, Devex: https://www.devex.com/news/inside-the-takedowns-of-ausaid-and-cida-85278.
3. Oxfam GB, How can UK aid pursue development and British National Interest at the same time? 2015: http://oxfamblogs.org/fp2p/how-can-uk-aid-pursue-development-and-british-national-interest-at-the-same-time/.
4. USAID, Mission, Vision and Values: https://www.usaid.gov/who-we-are/mission-vision-values.
5. Yifu Lin, Justin and Wang Yan, China's Contribution to Development Cooperation: Ideas, Opportunities and Financing in: Boussichas, Matthieu and Guillaumont, Patrick, Financing Sustainable Development Addressing Vulnerabilities, FERDI, 2015: http://www.ferdi.fr/sites/www.ferdi.fr/files/publication/fichiers/ferdi_-_financing_development-web-2_0.pdf.

6. Government of India Ministry of External Affairs: http://www.mea. gov.in/Speeches-Statements.htm?dtl/21549/Keynote+address+by +Foreign+Secretary+at+Conference+of+Southern+Providers+South-South+Cooperation++Issues+and+Emerging+Challenges.
7. Thanks to Simon Reid-Henry for some of the following analysis.
8. http://documents.worldbank.org/curated/en/297241468339565863/ World-development-report-1978.
9. Thanks to Simon Reid-Henry for most of this paragraph.

Bibliography

Alesina, A., & Dollar, D. (2000) Who gives foreign aid to whom and why? http://www.nber.org/papers/w6612.pdf

Alonso, J. A. (2017). From ODA to a new international development policy, April.

Alonso, J. A., Glennie, J., & Sumner, A. (2014). Recipients and contributors: Middle income countries and the future of development cooperation (DESA Working Paper No. 135, ST/ESA/2014/DWP/135). http://www.un.org/esa/desa/papers/2014/wp135_2014.pdf

Barder, O., & Birdsall, N. (2006). Payments for progress: A hands-off approach to foreign aid, Center for Global Development. http://www.cgdev.org/files/11550_file_12_1_06_Payments_for_Progress.pdf

Basu S. et al. (2012). An alternative mechanism for international health aid: Evaluating a Global Social Protection Fund.

Benn J., & Luijkx, W. (2017). Emerging providers' international co-operation for development, (April). http://www.oecd-ilibrary.org/content/workingpaper/15d6a3c7-en

Bhattacharya A. et al (2012). Infrastructure for development: Meeting the challenge. Centre for Climate Change Economics and Policy Grantham Research Institute on Climate Change and the Environment http://www.lse.ac.uk/GranthamInstitute/wp-content/uploads/2014/03/PP-infrastructure-for-development-meeting-the-challenge.pdf

Bordo M. et al. (2000) Financial Crises: Lessons from the last 120 years

Boussichas, M., & Guillaumont, P. (2015). Financing sustainable development addressing vulnerabilities, FERDI. http://www.ferdi.fr/sites/www.ferdi.fr/files/publication/fichiers/ferdi_-_financing_development-web-2_0.pdf

Canuto, O. (2015) Oil prices and the future of petrocaribe, The Huffington Post. http://www.huffingtonpost.com/otaviano-canuto/oil-prices-and-the-future_b_8209010.html

Carbonnier G. & Sumner A. (2012). Reframing aid in a world where the poor live in emerging economies.

Carothers T. & de Gramont D. (2013). Development Aid Confronts Politics: The Almost Revolution. Carnegie Endowment for International Peace.

CSEM. (2018). On the road to UHC: Leave no one behind. https://www.iapb. org/wp-content/uploads/on_the_road_to_uhc_csem_2018.pdf

de Cazotte, H. (2018). Seeking agreement on ODA, the UK, Germany and the US: Conclusions for France.

Development Committee (Joint Ministerial Committee of the Boards of Governors of the Bank and the Fund on the Transfer of Real Resources to Developing Countries). (2015). From Billions to Trillions: Transforming Development Finance Post-2015. https://siteresources.worldbank.org/DEVCOMMINT/ Documentation/23659446/DC2015-0002(E)FinancingforDevelopment.pdf

Development Initiatives. (2018). Investments to end poverty, meeting the financing challenge to leave no one behind. http://devinit.org/wp-content/ uploads/2018/12/Investments-to-End-Poverty-2018-Report.pdf

Di Ciommo M. (2014). Development Cooperation for the Future: The Increasing Role of Emerging Providers. Development Initiatives.

DIE. (2014). "Beyond Aid" and the future of development cooperation, April.

Dieleman J.L., et al. (2016). Development assistance for health: Past trends, associations, and the future of international financial flows for health.

Edward P. & Sumner A. (2013). The Geography of Inequality: Where and by How Much Has Income Distribution Changed since 1990? CGD Working Paper 341.

Eichengreen, B. (2010). Lessons from The Marshall Plan. http://web.worldbank. org/archive/website01306/web/pdf/wdr_2011_case_study_marshall_plan_1.pdf

Eurodad. (2014). Conditionally yours: An analysis of the policy conditions attached to IMF loans. http://www.eurodad.org/conditionallyyours

European Commission. (2014). An introduction to EU Cohesion Policy 2014– 2020. https://ec.europa.eu/regional_policy/sources/docgener/informat/basic/ basic_2014_en.pdf

European Commission. (2013). Beyond 2015: Towards a comprehensive and integrated approach to financing poverty eradication and sustainable development. http://ec.europa.eu/transparency/regdoc/rep/1/2013/EN/1-2013-531-EN-F1-1.Pdf

Fanon, F. (1961). The Wretched of the Earth.

Forbes. (2014). Ben Bernanke: The 2008 financial crisis was worse than the great depression. http://www.forbes.com/sites/timworstall/2014/08/27/ben-bernanke-the-2008-financial-crisis-was-worse-than-the-great-depression/

Gaspar V., et al. (2019). Fiscal Policy and Development. Spending Needs for Meeting Selected SDGs. IMF.

Glennie, J. (2008). The Trouble with Aid: Why less could mean more for Africa. Zed Books

Glennie, J. (2011). A research revolution to save the planet. www.guardian.co.uk/ global-development/poverty-matters/2011/jul/15/aid-money-research-clean-technology

Glennie J. et al. (2019). ODA, the next 50 years: A proposal for a new universal development commitment. https://www.wider.unu.edu/publication/ proposal-new-universal-development-commitment

Glennie J. & Hurley G. (2014a). Where next for aid post-2015, ODI and UNDP. http://www.undp.org/content/dam/undp/library/Poverty%20Reduction/Development%20Cooperation%20and%20Finance/UNDP-ODI–Where-Next-for-Aid-the-Post-2015-Opportunity-FINAL.pdf

Glennie J. & Hurley G. (2014b). https://www.theguardian.com/global-development/poverty-matters/2014/may/07/europe-aid-eu-middle-income-countries

Glennie J. & Prizzon A. (2012). From high to low aid: A proposal to classify countries by aid receipt, ODI. https://www.odi.org/publications/6383-high-low-aid-proposal-classify-countries-aid-receipt

Glennie J. & Sumner A. (2015). The Guardian. https://www.theguardian.com/global-development/2015/aug/05/aid-should-be-seen-as-foreign-public-investment-not-just-charity

Gómez-Reino, M. (2019). 'We first' and the Anti-foreign Aid Narratives, April.

Greening, J. (2013). Global trade can help us end the need for aid. https://www.gov.uk/government/speeches/justine-greening-global-trade-can-help-us-end-the-need-for-aid

Gulrajani, N. (2015). Dilemmas in donor design: Organisational reform and the future of foreign aid agencies, April.

Gulrajani, N., et al. (2019). The principled aid index: Understanding donor motivations, ODI. https://www.odi.org/publications/11294-principled-aid-index-understanding-donor-motivations

Gulrajani N. & Swiss L. (2019). Donorship in a State of Flux. ODI.

Hattori, T. (2001). Reconceptualising foreign aid. Review of International Political Economy. Vol. 8, No. 4 (Winter, 2001), pp. 633–660.

Hoeffler, A., &, Outram, V. (2008). Need, merit or self-interest – What determines the allocation of aid? http://www.csae.ox.ac.uk/workingpapers/pdfs/2008-19text.pdf

Hynes, W., &, Scott, S. (2013). "The evolution of official development assistance: Achievements, criticisms and a way forward", OECD Development Co-operation Working Papers, No. 12, OECD Publishing. http://dx.doi.org/10.1787/5k3v1dv3f024-en

IARAN. (2017). The Future of Aid: INGOs in 2030.

IDS. (2018). IDS Bulletin, July 2018, Emerging economies and the changing dynamics of development cooperation.

Inter-agency Task Force on Financing for Development. (2019). Financing for sustainable development report.

Kalu, K. (2018). Foreign Aid and the Future of Africa, April.

Kanbur R. & Sumner A. (2011). Poor Countries or Poor People? Development Assistance and the New Geography of Global Poverty, April.

Kaul, I. (2014). International public finance. https://www.ingekaul.net/wp-content/uploads/2014/01/International_Public_Financ_Fin.pdf

Kaul, I., & Conceição, P. (2006). The New Public Finance, Responding to Global Challenges.

Kenny C. (2011) Getting Better: Why Global Development Is Succeeding--And How We Can Improve the World Even More.

Killick T. (1998) Donor Conditionality and Policy Reform. In: Borner S., Paldam M. (eds) The Political Dimension of Economic Growth. International Economic Association Series. Palgrave Macmillan, London.

Killick, T. (2004, January). 'Politics, evidence and the new aid agenda', published in the Development Policy Review.

Manuel, M., et al. (2018). Financing the end of extreme poverty, ODI. https://www.odi.org/publications/11187-financing-end-extreme-poverty

Mawdsley, E. (2012). From Recipients to Donors, Emerging Powers and the Changing Development Landscape. Zed.

Mazzucato, M. (2011). The Entrepreneurial State: Debunking Public Vs. Private Sector Myths, April.

Mazzucato, M., Semieniuk, G., & Watson, J. (2015). What will it take to get us a Green Revolution? https://www.sussex.ac.uk/webteam/gateway/file.php?name=what-will-it-take-to-get-us-a-green-revolution.pdf&site=264

Mendez, R. (1992). International Public Finance. A New Perspective on Global Relations.

Moon S. & Omole O. (2017). Development assistance for health: Critiques, proposals and prospects for change, April.

Moyo, D. (2008). Dead Aid, Why Aid Is Not Working and How There Is Another Way for Africa. Penguin.

OECD. (2011). Divided we stand: Why inequality keeps rising. http://www.oecd.org/els/soc/dividedwestandwhyinequalitykeepsrising.htm

OECD. (2015). Multilateral aid 2015: Better partnerships for a post-2015 world: http://www.oecd.org/dac/multilateral-aid-2015-9789264235212-en.htm

OECD. (2015). Blended finance: A primer. http://www3.weforum.org/docs/WEF_Blended_Finance_A_Primer_Development_Finance_Philanthropic_Funders_report_2015.pdf

OECD & UNDP. (2019). Making development cooperation more effective, 2019 Progress Report. https://www.oecd.org/dac/making-development-co-operation-more-effective-26f2638f-en.htm

OECD et al. (2019), *Latin American Economic Outlook 2019: Development in Transition*, OECD Publishing, Paris, https://doi.org/10.1787/g2g9ff18-e

Olivié I. & Pérez A. (2019). Solidarity and security in the EU discourse on aid, April.

Ooms G., et al. (2010). Financing the Millennium Development Goals for health and beyond: sustaining the 'Big Push'.

Ooms G., et al. (2014). Beyond health aid: Would an international equalization scheme for universal health coverage serve the international collective interest?

Otterson T., et al. (2018). The challenge of middle-income countries to development assistance for health: Recipients, funders, both or neither?

Oxfam. (2019). Public Good or Private Wealth, https://www.oxfam.org/en/research/public-good-or-private-wealth.

Oxfam Australia. (2017). The future of Australian Aid, April.

Oxfam GB. (2015). How can UK aid pursue development and British National Interest at the same time? http://oxfamblogs.org/fp2p/how-can-uk-aid-pursue-development-and-british-national-interest-at-the-same-time/

Partos. (2018). Adapt, counteract or transform: The future of Dutch development cooperation. https://partos.nl/fileadmin/files/Documents/180411_Exploring_the_future_of_Dutch_development_cooperation.pdf

Pettifor A. (2019) The Case for the Green New Deal. Verso Books

Pezzini M. (2017). Development in transition. European Commission. https://ec.europa.eu/europeaid/sites/devco/files/op-ed-dit21-20170704_en.pdf

Pogge, T. (2015). The hunger games. https://papers.ssrn.com/sol3/papers.cfm?abstract_id=2823609

Ramalingan, B. (2013). Aid on the Edge of Chaos. Oxford.

Reid-Henry, S. (2016). Just global health? https://onlinelibrary.wiley.com/doi/abs/10.1111/dech.12245

Sachs J., et al. (2019). Closing the SDG Budget Gap.

Sagasti F., et al. (2004). Knowledge and Innovation for Development: The Sysiphys challenge of the 21st Century.

Sagasti F., et al (2005a). The Future of Development Financing: Challenges and Strategic Choices, New York, Palgrave Macmillan.

Sagasti, F. (2005a). Official development assistance: Background, context, issues and prospects. http://franciscosagasti.com/descargas/publicaciones_06/kkkk-sagasti-l20-oda-background-materials-dragged.pdf

SDSN. (2015). Partnerships and Investment Needs to Achieve the Sustainable Development Goals: Understanding the Billions and Trillions.

SDSN. (2015). Financing for Sustainable Development: Implementing the SDGs through Effective Investment Strategies.

SELA (2015) "Evolution of the PETROCARIBE Energy Cooperation Agreement." Permanent Secretariat of SELA, Caracas, Venezuela, June, SP/Di No. 6-15. http://www.sela.org/media/1950653/evolution-of-petrocaribe.pdf

Severino, J.-M., & Ray, O. (2009). The end of ODA: Death and rebirth of a global public policy, Center for Global Development. http://www.cgdev.org/sites/default/files/1421419_file_End_of_ODA_FINAL.pdf

Sharp, J. (2015). U.S. foreign aid to Israel. https://www.fas.org/sgp/crs/mideast/RL33222.pdf

Stern N., et al. (2013). A new world's new development bank. On Project Syndicate. http://www.project-syndicate.org/commentary/the-benefits-of-the-brics-development-bank

Stone, R. W. (2010). Buying Influence: Development Aid between the Cold War and the War on Terror, http://www.rochester.edu/College/PSC/stone/working_papers/buying_influence.pdf

Subramanian A. (2009). Aid, Dutch Disease and Manufacturing Growth. CGD Working Paper 196. https://papers.ssrn.com/sol3/papers.cfm?abstract_id=1542716

Summers, L. (2016). Keynote Address for Doha: The Future of Aid for Health, April.

Sumner, A. (2013), "Aid Agencies of the Future." The Economist, 3 June, http://www.economist.com/blogs/feastandfamine/2013/06/aid-agencies-future.

Troilo, P. (2015). Inside the takedowns of AusAID and CIDA, Devex. https://www.devex.com/news/inside-the-takedowns-of-ausaid-and-cida-85278

Vaes & Huyse. (2012). Development Cooperation in 2020? Hivos.

UNCTAD. (2015). Trade and development report. www.unctad.org/en/PublicationsLibrary/tdr2015_en.pdf

UNCTAD (2019) Trade and Development Report 2019: Financing a Global Green New Deal

UN DESA. (2012). World Economic and Social Survey 2012: In Search of New Development Finance. http://www.un.org/en/development/desa/policy/wess/wess_current/2012wess.pdf

UNDP. (2013). Human Development Report. The rise of the South: Human progress in a diverse world. http://hdr.undp.org/en/2013-report

UNDP. (2014). Start of KazAID marks significant transition in Kazakhstan from aid-recipient to donor. www.eurasia.undp.org/content/rbec/en/home/presscenter/articles/2014/11/3/start-kazaid-significant-transition-kazakhstan.html

UNDP. (2012). Innovative Financing for Development: A New Model for Development Finance? http://www.undp.org/content/undp/en/home/librarypage/poverty-reduction/development_cooperationandfinance/innovative_financingfor-developmentanewmodelfordevelopmentfinance.html

UN Millennium Project. (2005). Investing in development: A practical plan to achieve the Millennium Development Goals. https://www.who.int/hdp/publications/4b.pdf

United Nations MDG Gap Task Force Report 2015: Taking stock of the global partnership for development. http://www.un.org/en/development/desa/policy/mdg_gap/mdg_gap2015/2015GAP_FULLREPORT_EN.pdf

Wood B., et al. (2011). Evaluation of the Paris Declaration. https://www.oecd.org/derec/dacnetwork/48152078.pdf

Yanguas, P. (2018). Why We Lie About Aid, Development and the Messy Politics of Change. Zed Books.

Yun, S. (2014). China's aid to Africa: Monster or Messiah? www.brookings.edu/research/opinions/2014/02/07-china-aid-to-africa-sun

Index